Auto Repair for Beginners

The Ultimate Guide to Becoming Mechanically Independent: Fix Your Own Automobile Problems. Uncover the 15 Secrets to Keep Your Car Running Efficiently and Save Money. NEW 2024 EDITION

By Cooper Travis

Table Of Content

Introduction

The Road to Mechanical Independence

The freedom to drive is more than just a rite of passage; it's a symbol of independence. But this freedom doesn't stop with mastering the art of maneuvering a car. True vehicular independence comes from understanding the heart, soul, and anatomy of the machine you command. It's a journey towards mechanical independence—a path that allows you to not just drive, but also understand and care for your vehicle like the prized possession it truly is.

The Evolution of Our Relationship with Cars

In the early days of automobiles, cars were a luxury, a marvel of engineering reserved for the elite. The majority of owners back then were closely acquainted with their car's inner workings, often out of necessity. With limited mechanics and services available, understanding the basics was crucial.

Over time, as cars became a staple in households and their designs more intricate, a significant portion of drivers lost that intimate connection with their vehicles. We started relying more on mechanics and specialists, and while there's undeniable value in expert knowledge, we lost a piece of our mechanical independence in the process.

Today, we're on the precipice of change. With resources at our fingertips and an ever-growing DIY culture, we're slowly reclaiming our mechanical autonomy. But why is this road to independence so essential?

Empowerment through Understanding

Imagine the confidence that comes from not being at the mercy of warning lights on your dashboard, or the assurance from recognizing when a strange noise is a simple fix versus a sign of a deeper problem. This empowerment doesn't just save you money; it transforms the way you interact with your vehicle.

When you understand your car's needs and nuances, you experience a sense of connection. Like a trusted steed from tales of old, your vehicle becomes an extension of you. This bond enhances your driving experience, making every journey not just about reaching a destination, but also about enjoying the voyage itself.

Not Just a Machine, But a Partner

Think back to a time when you faced adversity. Maybe it was a flat tire on a stormy night, or the unsettling rumble of an engine in a deserted parking lot. In those moments, our cars can feel like adversaries. But with mechanical knowledge, the dynamic changes. Your vehicle shifts from being just a machine to a partner, working with you to overcome challenges.

For instance, knowing the signs of a failing battery could mean the difference between getting stranded or making it to safety. Recognizing the importance of timely oil changes can prolong your car's life, turning a potential liability into a lasting asset.

The Beauty of Autonomy and Trust

Mechanical independence isn't about replacing your mechanic or becoming an expert overnight. It's about striking a balance between trust and autonomy. It's understanding when to roll up your sleeves and when to seek expertise.

Trust in this context works two-fold. There's the trust you place in professionals, a valuable and necessary aspect of car ownership. And then there's trust in yourself, your judgment, and your ability to understand and care for your vehicle.

Setting the Stage for Your Journey

The road to mechanical independence is paved with curiosity, a touch of bravery, and a desire to learn. As we delve deeper into this guide, you'll discover the intricacies of your vehicle's anatomy, the secrets of preventative maintenance, and the nuances of its various systems.

By the end, you won't just be a driver; you'll be an informed car enthusiast, armed with the knowledge to care for your vehicle and appreciate its marvels.

In this journey, you're not alone. We'll navigate this path together, ensuring every twist and turn is a step closer to making you and your car true partners on the road.

Chapter 1: The Anatomy of Your Vehicle

Essential Components and Their Functions

Much like our own bodies, vehicles possess a complexity that might seem overwhelming at first glance. But, as we peel back the layers, a symphony of interconnected parts working in harmony reveals itself. Every component, large or small, plays a crucial role in ensuring your car delivers its best performance, safety, and comfort.

The Heartbeat: The Engine

At the center of it all is the engine, the beating heart of your car. It's where fuel meets air, and with a spark, they combust to produce power. This energy then propels your vehicle forward. But the engine is not just about raw power; it's a masterpiece of precision and timing. Every valve, piston, and belt must synchronize perfectly to keep your car humming along.

Imagine sitting by a serene lake, skimming stones. The force, angle, and spin you apply dictate how well the stone skips. Similarly, the engine balances multiple factors to ensure efficiency. Too much fuel and not enough air might flood the system, while the inverse could strain the engine.

Car's Respiratory System: The Air Intake and Exhaust

Just as we inhale oxygen and exhale carbon dioxide, your car breathes too. The air intake system ensures a steady supply of fresh air, which is vital for the combustion process in the engine. On the flip side, the exhaust system expels used gases, making room for fresh air.

It's akin to exercising. Imagine jogging: you control your breathing, take in fresh air, and exhale the old. Your car does the same, maintaining a balance to keep its engine healthy.

Quenching the Thirst: The Cooling System

Have you ever sprinted on a hot day and felt the need to hydrate and cool down? Your car, too, feels the heat, especially with all the intense internal reactions. The cooling system, including the radiator, ensures the engine doesn't overheat.

It circulates coolant, absorbing and dissipating heat to maintain optimal operating temperatures.

If you've ever sipped a cold beverage on a sweltering day, you understand the importance of cooling down. It's not just about comfort but about maintaining balance and ensuring longevity.

Lifeblood Circulation: The Oil System

Our joints need lubrication to move smoothly. Similarly, the numerous moving parts in an engine require lubrication to prevent wear and tear. The oil system circulates this lubricant, ensuring every moving part slides smoothly without excessive friction.

Recall the soothing relief of applying a moisturizer to dry skin. This is the solace the oil system provides to the engine, ensuring every journey is smooth and wear-free.

The Nervous System: Sensors and Controls

Just as our nervous system provides vital feedback to our brain, a modern car is equipped with a myriad of sensors. These sensors monitor everything from oxygen levels in the exhaust to the temperature of the engine, sending data to the car's computer. This feedback loop allows the car to make real-time adjustments to optimize performance and efficiency.

Think of when you touch something hot. Instantly, your brain processes the pain and signals your hand to retract. Cars, too, adjust instantly, ensuring they're always operating in peak conditions.

Muscles in Motion: The Transmission

Muscles give our bodies motion, and in cars, the transmission plays a similar role. It takes power from the engine and transfers it to the wheels, allowing the car to move. The transmission ensures this power delivery is smooth, shifting gears as necessary based on speed and load.

It's like changing your pace from a walk to a jog, then to a sprint. Each pace requires a different gait and rhythm. The transmission ensures your car always finds its optimal rhythm.

Defensive Line: The Brakes

Safety is paramount, and while the engine propels the car forward, the brakes ensure it can stop safely. Using a combination of hydraulic fluids, mechanical components, and friction materials, the braking system slows down the vehicle and brings it to a halt.

Consider it akin to the brakes in our own lives—the moments of pause, reflection, and rest. Just as we sometimes need to stop, reassess, or simply take a break, our vehicles need an effective way to halt their momentum, especially in unforeseen circumstances.

The Art of Direction: Steering and Suspension

Steering gives direction, while the suspension ensures that direction is smooth and comfortable. Together, they make driving a tactile and responsive experience. The steering system interprets your inputs from the wheel, turning the car's wheels in the desired direction. Meanwhile, the suspension system absorbs road imperfections, providing a smoother ride. Imagine navigating a dance floor. Your eyes and intent (the steering) guide your steps, while your body's flexibility (the suspension) allows you to glide smoothly, even when the floor might be uneven.

The Protector: The Chassis and Body

Sheltering all these vital components is the car's body and chassis. It doesn't just define the aesthetic appeal of your vehicle but also provides structural integrity and safety. Reinforced zones absorb impacts, crumple zones reduce crash energy, and the overall design ensures aerodynamic efficiency.

This is the protective shell, akin to our own skin and bones. Just as our skin shields us from external factors and our skeletal system provides structure, the car's body is its first line of defense against the outside world.

Fueling the Fire: The Fuel System

Every living being needs nourishment, and for cars, it's fuel. The fuel system stores and supplies the engine with the necessary gasoline or diesel to produce power. From the fuel tank to the injectors, every component ensures that the engine receives a precise mixture for optimal combustion. Imagine preparing a meal: you need the right ingredients in the correct proportions to create a culinary masterpiece. Similarly, the fuel system ensures your engine gets its perfect meal every time it ignites.

Electrifying the Spirit: The Electrical System

While we'll dive deeper into this in another chapter, it's essential to touch upon the fact that modern cars heavily rely on electricity. From igniting the engine to powering your infotainment system, the electrical grid in your vehicle is the silent force behind many conveniences and functionalities.

Think of it as the spark in our lives, the zest and energy. Just as our spirit or mood can light up a room, the electrical system illuminates and energizes many aspects of our cars.

Gazing Ahead: The Lighting System
Night or day, clear or foggy, our cars need to see and be seen. The lighting system, including headlights, taillights, and indicators, ensures visibility in all conditions. These lights communicate our intentions to other drivers and light our path in the darkness.
It's the guiding light in our journey, much like a lighthouse for ships or a lantern in the olden days—ensuring we traverse safely, no matter the external conditions.

Electrical Systems Demystified

In a world teeming with electronic gadgets and devices, our vehicles have not been left behind. Today's cars have evolved into highly sophisticated machines, where electrical systems control and support a vast number of operations. From the gentle chime that reminds you to buckle your seatbelt to the complex navigational aids that guide you to your destination, electricity is the invisible force guiding countless processes within your vehicle.

Harnessing Nature's Power: The Car Battery

At the heart of any electrical system lies a power source, and for most vehicles, this source is the car battery. This unassuming box, typically nestled under the hood, is a reservoir of electrical energy. Its primary role? To start your car by powering the starter motor and ignition system. Once the car is running, the battery also supplies power to other electrical components as needed.

It's much like the charged atmosphere just before a rainstorm, filled with potential and waiting to be unleashed. A car without a functioning battery is much like a storm that never breaks – full of potential but unable to spring into action.

A Dance of Charge and Discharge: The Alternator

If the battery is the reservoir of power, the alternator is the diligent worker ensuring it stays filled. As your vehicle runs, the alternator continuously recharges the battery, ensuring it's ready for the next engine start. Beyond this, the alternator supplies power to the vehicle's electrical systems when the car is running, taking the load off the battery.

Think of the alternator as a diligent bee, buzzing from flower to flower, gathering nectar and ensuring the hive's sustenance. It works behind the scenes, ensuring the battery, the hive of your car's electrical world, remains nourished and thriving.

Wires, Fuses, and Relays: The Circulatory System of Your Car

Much like our veins and arteries transport life-giving blood, a complex web of wires, fuses, and relays distribute power throughout the vehicle. Fuses act as protective barriers, breaking the circuit if there's an overload, much like circuit breakers in our homes.

Relays, on the other hand, are like traffic signals, ensuring power flows in the correct direction and to the right components.

Imagine a bustling city, with its intricate network of roads, bridges, and traffic lights, ensuring smooth flow and preventing chaos. This is precisely the role of your car's electrical circulatory system, directing the flow of electricity, ensuring efficiency, and preventing potential hazards.

Sensing and Adjusting: The Role of Sensors

Our modern cars are not just about power; they are about finesse, adaptability, and intelligence. Embedded within the vehicle are numerous sensors, constantly monitoring various parameters. From checking engine temperature and oxygen levels in the exhaust to measuring tire pressure, these sensors provide real-time data, allowing the vehicle's onboard computer to make instantaneous adjustments.

Consider these sensors as the ever-watchful eyes and ears of your car, akin to our senses that continuously gather information, allowing us to react, adapt, and navigate our surroundings.

Command and Control: The Onboard Computer

With a plethora of sensors generating a constant stream of data, there needs to be a central processing hub. Enter the onboard computer, the brain of your vehicle. It interprets data from the sensors, making split-second decisions that can affect performance, safety, and efficiency. Adjusting fuel mixture, managing the anti-lock braking system, or even tweaking the air conditioner's output, the onboard computer seamlessly integrates the demands of modern driving.

Reflect upon the marvel of our human brain, rapidly processing stimuli, and guiding our reactions. Similarly, the onboard computer ensures your car remains a step ahead, ready to tackle any challenge the road presents.

The Interface of Experience: Dashboard and Infotainment

The dashboard and infotainment system are your interfaces with your car's electrical world. The dashboard, with its array of lights, gauges, and indicators, provides crucial feedback on the vehicle's status. Meanwhile, the infotainment system caters to entertainment, navigation, and connectivity needs.

Remember the thrill of an interactive exhibit at a museum, where information and feedback are immediate? Your dashboard and infotainment system are akin to this, bridging the gap between driver and machine, ensuring a harmonious journey filled with knowledge and enjoyment.

Types of Vehicles: From Sedans to SUVs

The open road beckons and offers promises of adventure, opportunities, and unforgettable experiences. But how we tread on this road, in what kind of vehicle, adds a different flavor to each journey. In the intricate world of automotives, the diversity of vehicles caters to various needs, preferences, and lifestyles. Each type of vehicle tells a story, has a purpose, and serves a unique audience.

Sedans: The Timeless Classic

For decades, the sedan has been the epitome of class, practicality, and understated elegance. With a distinct three-box configuration – the engine compartment, passenger compartment, and the trunk – sedans are often the first choice for those seeking comfort and functionality. They glide seamlessly through city streets, offering spacious interiors and a balanced driving experience. Whether you're a business professional or a family-oriented individual, sedans often strike the right chord between luxury and practicality.

Imagine the sedate rhythm of a waltz – elegant, timeless, and graceful. That's the essence of a sedan on the open road.

Hatchbacks: The Energetic Urbanite

Compact, versatile, and zesty – hatchbacks are the lively dancers of the automotive world. With their truncated rear end and a door that swings upwards, hatchbacks offer a combination of compact design and storage versatility. They are the favorites among city dwellers, who need to navigate through narrow lanes and tight parking spaces. Their spirited nature and adaptable storage make them ideal for both quick errands and weekend getaways.

Think of the vibrant beats of a salsa, rhythmic and full of energy. That's the hatchback, always ready for a spontaneous adventure.

SUVs: The Robust Adventurers

Sport Utility Vehicles (SUVs) exude strength, capability, and a promise of adventures beyond the city limits. With a high ground clearance, a robust build, and often equipped with all-wheel drive, SUVs are designed for those who don't want to be confined by the boundaries of paved roads. Whether it's a mountain trail, a desert terrain, or snowy paths, SUVs assert dominance and ensure a comfortable journey, no matter the landscape.

Imagine the powerful performance of a tribal dance, resonating with strength and passion. That's the SUV, unyielding and ready to conquer any terrain.

Coupes: The Stylish Performers
Sleek, low-slung, and often with just two doors, coupes are the automotive embodiment of style and performance. These vehicles are for those who love the thrill of speed, the allure of a distinctive design, and the symphony of a roaring engine. While they might not be the most practical choice for large families, coupes appeal to the enthusiast, the connoisseur, the individual who sees driving not just as a commute but as an art.
Picture the precision and flair of a tango – intense, captivating, and deeply passionate. That's the coupe, turning every drive into a performance.

Convertibles: The Free Spirits
With roofs that fold down or retract, convertibles offer an unobstructed view of the sky. They are for those who wish to break free, feel the wind in their hair, and embrace the world without barriers. Convertibles are not just vehicles; they are experiences, an assertion of freedom and a celebration of the joy of driving.
Imagine the liberated movements of contemporary dance – uninhibited, expressive, and open. That's the convertible, inviting you to a journey under the open heavens.

Minivans: The Family Maestros
Designed with family in mind, minivans are spacious, practical, and equipped with features that cater to both the young and old. Sliding doors, multiple rows of seats, and various entertainment options make minivans the preferred choice for those with larger families or those who prioritize space and convenience over everything else.
Think of the coordinated steps of a group dance, where every movement is synchronized, and everyone has a place. That's the minivan, ensuring every family member travels in comfort and harmony.

Chapter 2: The Power of Preventative Maintenance

The Lifespan Extension Benefits

There's a profound adage that says, "An ounce of prevention is worth a pound of cure." It's a principle that rings true not only in health and relationships but also in the automotive world. You see, vehicles, much like living beings, have a rhythm, a heartbeat, and when tended to with care, they reward us with longevity, performance, and the whispered tales of many journeys.

Understanding the Lifespan of a Vehicle

Before we dive into the vast ocean of benefits that preventative maintenance brings, let's pause for a moment to understand what we mean by 'lifespan' in the context of a vehicle. It isn't just about the number of years or miles a car can run; it's about the quality of those years and miles. It's the difference between a vehicle that limps along, constantly plagued by issues, and one that roars to life with every ignition, ready to face the adventures of the road.

The Hidden Symphony of Care

Economic Euphony

One of the most immediate and tangible benefits of regular preventative maintenance is the financial savings. When you address minor issues before they evolve into major problems, you're not just saving on potential repair costs; you're also safeguarding the intricate web of interconnected components that comprise your vehicle. For instance, ensuring that your brake pads are replaced when needed can prevent more extensive damage to the brake rotors, which are significantly more expensive to replace.

Moreover, a well-maintained vehicle has a higher resale value. When the time comes to part ways with your trusty companion, the meticulous care you've provided over the years will be evident, enticing potential buyers and commanding a better price.

Performance Poetry

Every driver knows the sheer joy of a smooth ride – the hum of the engine, the grip of the tires on the road, the responsive embrace of the steering wheel. Regular maintenance ensures that this symphony of movement remains harmonious. By regularly changing the oil, for example, you ensure that the engine runs smoothly, reducing wear and tear and ensuring optimal fuel efficiency.

Furthermore, simple acts, like keeping the tires inflated to the recommended pressure, can drastically improve the vehicle's performance. It ensures even tire wear, better fuel economy, and a smoother, safer ride.

Safety Sonata

In the grand composition of automotive benefits, safety stands as the most solemn and crucial note. Vehicles are marvels of engineering, designed to protect and transport. But their ability to do so diminishes when they're not in optimal condition. Preventative maintenance isn't just about prolonging the life of your vehicle; it's about preserving the lives of its occupants.

Routine checks of the braking system, the lights, and the suspension, among others, ensure that the vehicle responds accurately in emergency situations, providing that extra moment or maneuver that can prevent accidents.

Environmental Enchantment

We live in an age of increasing environmental consciousness, where every action and its impact on our planet are scrutinized. Vehicles, by their nature, have an environmental footprint. However, a well-maintained vehicle minimizes this impact. Reduced emissions, better fuel efficiency, and decreased waste from broken parts are but a few of the eco-friendly benefits of regular maintenance.

Routine Checks and Their Impact

Many of life's most profound moments happen in the subtleties. It's the almost imperceptible shift in the wind before a storm, the faintest hue at dawn signaling a new day. Similarly, the intricate dance of mechanics within your vehicle often whispers its needs before shouting them, and it's in our best interest to listen intently. Routine checks act as our ears to these whispers, allowing us to address concerns when they're mere murmurs, rather than waiting for them to become roaring issues.

The Underlying Rhythms of Routine Checks

Setting the Pace: Establishing a Timeline
Understanding when to check is as vital as knowing what to check. While every vehicle and its usage patterns are unique, a general guideline for routine checks can be established. For instance, oil changes are typically suggested every 3,000 to 5,000 miles, but if you're using synthetic oil or if your manufacturer recommends longer intervals, this can change. Tire rotations might be needed every six months or 6,000 miles. By adhering to a dedicated timeline, you're ensuring the vibrancy of the vehicle's performance.

The Fluidity of Life
Just as our bodies rely on fluids like blood and water to function, so does your vehicle. Motor oil, transmission fluid, brake fluid, coolant, and power steering fluid are the lifeblood of your car. Their levels and quality can provide keen insights into the health of your automobile. For example, if you consistently notice a drop in engine oil levels, it might be indicative of a leak or increased oil consumption, signaling that it's time for a deeper inspection.

Bringing Light to Darkness: Illumination Checks
It's not just about seeing but also being seen. Regularly checking your vehicle's lights ensures not only that you have a clear vision during nighttime or adverse weather conditions but also that other motorists can see you. This simple act dramatically amplifies safety, making sure you're not just a ghostly apparition on a fog-laden highway.

The Grounded Reality: Tire Assessments

Tires are where your vehicle kisses the earth. They're the point of contact, the mediator between machine and terrain. Regularly assessing the tire pressure, tread depth, and overall condition can make a marked difference in fuel efficiency, ride smoothness, and safety. A tire with worn-out treads can be disastrous in wet conditions, and one that's under-inflated might affect fuel economy and handling.

Harnessing Harmony: Belts and Hoses

While they might not be the stars of the automotive show, belts and hoses play critical supporting roles. They ensure that various components of your vehicle synchronize harmoniously. A broken timing belt, for instance, can spell disaster for your engine. Regular inspections can help identify signs of wear or potential weak points, allowing for timely replacements and averting potential breakdowns.

The Symphony of Consequences

There's a ripple effect to routine checks, a series of consequences that cascade from the act of simple inspections. Firstly, there's the immediate benefit of averting potential issues, translating to savings and safety. But then there's the cumulative impact. Over time, a well-maintained vehicle demands fewer major repairs. The engine runs smoother, the brakes respond better, and the ride feels more controlled.

Beyond the tangible, there's an emotional peace that comes with knowing you're in a vehicle that's cared for. It's the comfort of reliability, the assurance that when you turn the ignition, the car will respond with gusto, ready to accompany you on your journey, be it to a nearby grocery store or a cross-country adventure.

Unmasking the Long-term Benefits

In the midst of our busy lives, we sometimes fail to recognize the behind-the-scenes elements that play pivotal roles. Just as the roots of a tree nourish its visible parts, routine checks and preventative maintenance provide unseen yet indispensable support to your car's performance and longevity. However, understanding the broader scope of these actions can shine a light on the long-term benefits that truly shape the relationship between an individual and their vehicle.

Invest Now, Save Later: The Economics of Forethought

Pocketbook Perks

At first glance, spending money on routine checks might seem like an avoidable expense. Why fix what's not broken, right? However, the counterintuitive magic of maintenance is that it's a financial safeguard. Addressing minor issues before they escalate not only spares you larger repair bills down the line but also extends the lifespan of car parts and the vehicle itself. Over time, these savings compound. Think of it as investing in stock: small, regular contributions can lead to significant returns over the years.

Fuel Efficiency: The Quiet Saver

A well-maintained vehicle runs smoother, and a smoother-running vehicle is more fuel-efficient. Whether it's ensuring your tires are correctly inflated or keeping the engine well-lubricated with timely oil changes, these activities optimize your car's fuel consumption. Over the lifespan of a vehicle, this can translate to substantial savings at the gas pump.

Safety First, Always: The Lifeguard of Maintenance

There's no price tag on safety. Ensuring that brakes are responsive, tires have adequate tread, and lights function as intended, translates to a safer driving experience. This not only reduces the risk of accidents but also provides the driver with the confidence to handle various road conditions. The peace of mind knowing your vehicle won't betray you in a critical moment is invaluable.

A Symphony of Harmony: Prolonged Performance Peaks

When each part of a machine works in unison, the result is harmonious and optimized performance. Through regular checks and maintenance, each component of your vehicle gets the attention it deserves. This means less wear and tear and an engine that purrs rather than growls. The end product? A ride that feels as good as new, year after year.

Maintaining Value: Financial and Sentimental

Cars, like homes, can be both a financial investment and a container of memories. A well-maintained vehicle holds its value better, fetching a higher resale price when the time comes to part ways. But beyond the monetary, there's a sentimental value. The family trips, the late-night drives, the milestones marked - each of these memories is sweeter in a car that's been cared for and cherished.

Sustainability: The Environment Thanks You

In an age of environmental awareness, it's essential to recognize the ecological impact of our choices. A well-maintained car emits fewer pollutants, ensuring cleaner air and a reduced carbon footprint. By being diligent about your vehicle's health, you're not only taking care of your immediate surroundings but also contributing to global well-being.

Chapter 3: The Heartbeat: Engine Repair & Maintenance

Key Engine Components

When you listen to the purr of your car, what you're truly tuning into is the rhythm of its heart: the engine. This powerhouse not only gives life to your vehicle but also shapes the very essence of your driving experience. By exploring the key components of this mechanical marvel, we embark on a journey to understand its intricate operations and the symphony of parts working in tandem.

The Chamber of Life: The Combustion Chamber

Just as our heart chambers pump blood, the combustion chamber of an engine is where the magic truly happens. This is the space where fuel and air combine, ignite, and produce the energy that sets your car in motion. The design and efficiency of this chamber influence power, fuel efficiency, and emissions. It's like a stage where every performance can be electrifying, given the right mix and timing.

The Breath of the Beast: Valves and Cams

Every engine needs to breathe. Enter valves and cams. The intake valves inhale the air-fuel mixture while the exhaust valves exhale the burned gases out. Acting like the maestro of this breathing process, the camshaft ensures that the valves open and close at the precise moments, choreographing a dance that fuels motion. The rhythmic up and down of these valves, controlled by the camshaft, is the essence of the engine's respiratory system.

The Pulse Driver: The Piston and Cylinder

If the combustion chamber is the heart, then the pistons and cylinders are its beating pulse. The piston moves within the cylinder, converting the energy from the ignited fuel-air mix into mechanical force. This movement, a constant dance of descent and ascent, drives the crankshaft and ultimately powers the wheels. The harmonious relationship between the piston and cylinder is fundamental for a smooth drive.

The Twisting Force: The Crankshaft

The crankshaft is the backbone of your engine, translating the vertical movement of the pistons into rotational force that drives your wheels. Think of it as the rod that turns the skipping of your heart into the rhythm of your steps. Its strength and balance are paramount, ensuring that every pulse of energy is efficiently transferred.

Lifeblood Flow: The Oil System

Like our circulatory system carries blood, the engine's oil system circulates lubrication, ensuring smooth operation, minimizing wear, and carrying away heat. The oil pump, filter, and pan collectively ensure that this lifeblood reaches every nook and cranny. The fluidity and consistency with which this system works can be likened to the way our veins and arteries maintain our vitality.

Cool Under Pressure: The Cooling System

Engines are fiery beasts, and they can get hot. Really hot. The cooling system, comprising the radiator, thermostat, water pump, and a network of hoses, ensures that this heat doesn't become destructive. By circulating coolant and regulating its flow, this system ensures that the engine maintains an optimal temperature, much like how our body sweats to cool down.

Taking Charge: The Timing Belt

Timing is everything. The timing belt, often unsung, maintains the synchronicity between the crankshaft and the camshaft, ensuring that valves and pistons move in harmony. A slip in this timing can be catastrophic, emphasizing the importance of this rubbery ring. It's the conductor, ensuring every section of the orchestra plays in unison.

Breathing Out: The Exhaust System

After the energy is extracted from the air-fuel mixture, the residual gases need an exit. The exhaust system, culminating in the tailpipe, ensures these gases are expelled efficiently and safely, all the while reducing noise and pollutants. It's the engine's way of exhaling after a deep breath, making way for the next cycle.

The Guardian: The Engine Control Unit (ECU)
In an age of technology, the ECU is the brain behind the brawn. This computerized unit oversees and adjusts engine operations, optimizing performance and efficiency. It's the guardian angel, continuously monitoring and making minute adjustments, ensuring the engine runs at its best.

Operational Fundamentals of Engines

The heart of any vehicle, the engine, isn't just a machine; it's a beautifully orchestrated symphony where every component plays a distinct note. While we've looked at the individual instruments in the previous section, it's crucial to understand the music they create together. Welcome to the operational fundamentals of engines, where science meets poetry.

The Four-Act Ballet: The Four-Stroke Cycle
Engines operate in a cyclical ballet, known commonly as the four-stroke cycle. It's a continuous dance of intake, compression, combustion, and exhaust. But what does that mean?

Intake: The First Breath
Imagine taking a deep breath, filling your lungs with air. The intake stroke is the engine's inhalation. As the piston moves down in the cylinder, the intake valve opens, allowing a mixture of fuel and air to rush in, filling the combustion chamber. This is the preparation, the anticipation before the crescendo.

Compression: Building The Tension
After that preparatory inhalation comes the compression. The piston begins its upward journey, compressing the fuel-air mixture as all valves close, sealing the chamber. It's akin to the tension in the air before a thunderstorm, the momentary silence before a musical climax.

Combustion: Release and Energy
The climax of our engine ballet! A spark from the spark plug ignites the compressed fuel-air mix, causing an explosion. This explosion forces the piston down with tremendous power, producing the energy that propels the vehicle forward. It's the exhilarating rush of a rollercoaster's descent or the peak of a musical chorus.

Exhaust: The Calming Exhale
After the rush of combustion, the engine needs to exhale, releasing the used gases to make room for the next cycle. The exhaust valve opens as the piston rises again, pushing out the burnt gases. This is the calm after the storm, the gentle exhale after a hearty laugh, resetting the stage for the dance to begin anew.

The Heartbeat's Rhythm: Engine RPM
RPM, or Revolutions Per Minute, is a measure of how frequently the engine's cycle repeats itself in a minute. It's the pulse, the rhythm of our engine's heartbeat. A faster RPM means more power but also signifies more wear and stress on the engine components. Like the tempo in music, it sets the pace for the journey.

Fueling the Fire: The Role of the Fuel Injector
In modern engines, the fuel injector plays a pivotal role, replacing old carburetors. It sprays fuel into the combustion chamber in a fine mist, ensuring efficient and complete burning. Think of it as the maestro, ensuring each instrument (in this case, droplet) plays its part perfectly.

Breathing Right: The Importance of Air-to-Fuel Ratio
For optimal combustion, an engine requires the right mix of air and fuel. Too much fuel and not enough air can lead to incomplete combustion, while too much air can cause the engine to run hot. This balance, often managed by the Engine Control Unit (ECU), ensures efficient operation and minimizes emissions. It's the delicate balance between the notes and silence in a melody.

The Oil's Embrace: Lubrication and Protection
We've spoken about the oil system, but its role in engine operation can't be overstated. By reducing friction and carrying away heat, it ensures the engine's components move smoothly and don't wear out prematurely. The oil is like the gentle hand guiding the dancers, ensuring they glide gracefully without stumbling.

Lubrication System

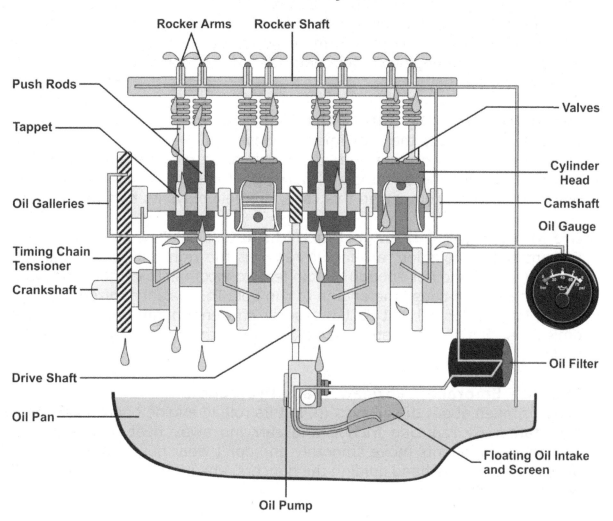

Rocker Arms   Rocker Shaft

Push Rods

Tappet

Oil Galleries

Timing Chain Tensioner

Crankshaft

Drive Shaft

Oil Pan

Oil Pump

Valves

Cylinder Head

Camshaft

Oil Gauge

Oil Filter

Floating Oil Intake and Screen

Engine Diagnostics and Troubleshooting

An engine, much like any living being, has its unique way of communicating. Whether it's a light tapping sound, a series of flashes on the dashboard, or even an unusual scent, these are the engine's way of crying out for attention. And just as a doctor diagnoses a patient's symptoms to understand the ailment, so too must we learn the art of engine diagnostics and troubleshooting.

The Dashboard: Your Car's Health Report
The dashboard of a car isn't just for show. Those blinking lights and gauges are the first line of communication between your engine and you. A check engine light might be a mystery at first glance, but with modern tools like OBD (On-Board Diagnostics) scanners, even the most perplexing of signals can be deciphered.
For instance, a steadily glowing engine light might point to emission problems or a loose gas cap, while a blinking light might hint at more severe issues, like a misfire that could damage the catalytic converter.

Sounds and Vibrations: Feeling the Distress
Your car's engine shouldn't sound like a rock band's drummer during a solo. A smooth purr is what you're aiming for. However, sounds like knocks, pings, or excessive idling can be indicative of various problems:

- **Knocks:** Often a result of the air-to-fuel mixture in the cylinders being detonated prematurely. It's not just an annoying sound; it can be harmful to the engine if ignored.

- **Squeals:** Typically related to belt issues. It might be a sign that a belt is loose or worn out.

- **Rough Idling:** If your car feels jumpy while it's stationary, it could hint at problems with spark plugs or perhaps a clogged fuel line.

Smoke Signals: What the Exhaust is Telling You
The color of the smoke from your exhaust can reveal a lot about what might be wrong:

- **White Smoke:** Often points to coolant entering the combustion chamber. You might be looking at a blown head gasket or a cracked engine block.

- **Blue Smoke:** Indicates oil burning alongside fuel. Potential culprits could be worn valve seals or damaged piston rings.

- **Black Smoke:** Suggests the engine is burning an excessive amount of fuel, possibly due to a clogged air filter or a malfunctioning sensor.

A Nose for Trouble: Sniffing Out Engine Issues
Unusual smells can be as telling as any dashboard light:

- **Rotten Eggs:** This unpleasant aroma might mean a problem with the catalytic converter.

- **Gasoline:** If you catch a whiff after a failed start, it's likely the engine is flooded with fuel.

- **Sweet Syrup:** Often signifies a coolant leak.

The Feel of the Road: Navigating Using Your Hands and Feet
Sometimes, the clues come from how the car responds to your actions:

- **Sluggish Acceleration:** Could be a sign of clogged fuel lines or a malfunctioning accelerator pump.

- **Shaking Steering Wheel:** Might indicate unbalanced tires, or more ominously, issues with the vehicle's driveline.

Modern Tech: OBD Scanners and Advanced Diagnostics
For those mysteries that aren't easily solved through senses alone, technology comes to the rescue. Modern cars come equipped with computer systems that monitor and manage various aspects of vehicle operation. An OBD scanner can be plugged into most vehicles, giving a detailed error report, pinpointing issues, and providing a starting point for repairs.

Top 10 Engine Care Tips for Optimal Performance

The engine, a marvel of modern engineering, is often regarded as the heart of any vehicle. Its rhythmic beats and harmonious roars bring life to our cars. Yet, like any precious entity, it requires tender love and care to continue performing at its peak. While understanding its ailments is essential, preventing these ailments in the first place is the true art of engine care. Dive with me into the realm of proactive engine maintenance, where we uncover the ten cardinal rules for optimal engine performance.

1. Regular Oil Changes: The Lifeline of Your Engine

Oil is to an engine what blood is to our bodies. It lubricates, cools, and cleans, ensuring the engine's smooth operation. Regular oil changes, as recommended in your car's manual, prevent the accumulation of sludge and debris. Opt for high-quality engine oil; consider it an investment in your vehicle's future.

2. Keep it Cool: Maintain the Cooling System

Overheating is a silent engine killer. Ensuring the radiator is free of leaks, the coolant is fresh, and the thermostat functions flawlessly, guarantees that your engine remains at an optimal temperature. Remember, an engine that stays cool stays powerful.

3. Breathe Easy: Clean Air Filters for Clear Performance

An engine breathes, drawing in air to aid in the combustion process. A clogged or dirty air filter restricts this airflow, leading to reduced efficiency and increased fuel consumption. Changing air filters routinely is like gifting your engine a fresh breath of mountain air.

4. Quality Fuel: The Premium Choice

Not all fuels are created equal. Opting for a higher octane rating or cleaner fuel might come at a slightly higher price but pays dividends in engine performance and longevity. Remember, it's not just about filling up; it's about filling up right.

5. Belt Check: The Unsung Heroes

Belts drive various engine components, from alternators to water pumps. A worn-out or loose belt can impair engine functions or, worse, snap unexpectedly.

Periodic inspections ensure these silent soldiers continue marching in perfect order.

6. Timely Tune-Ups: Calibration is Key
Engines aren't set-it-and-forget-it systems. They require regular tune-ups to adjust elements like spark plugs, fuel injectors, and more. An engine in tune is music not only to the ears but also to the soul of your vehicle.

7. Battery Health: Ignite the Spark
While not a direct engine component, the battery is the source of that initial spark that brings the engine to life. Ensure your battery is free from corrosion, the terminals are tight, and the charge is optimal. A healthy battery ensures an engine that roars to life at the first turn of the key.

8. The Right Pressure: Not Just for Tires
We often associate pressure checks with tires, but the engine's fuel pressure is equally crucial. A malfunctioning fuel pump or a clogged fuel filter can starve the engine of its essential nourishment. Periodic checks ensure the fuel flows freely, just as nature intended.

9. Listen Actively: Your Engine Talks
The art of listening goes a long way. Regularly running your engine and tuning into its sounds can help detect anomalies before they magnify. A slight knock or a hiss might be your engine's way of whispering its troubles.

10. Professional Gaze: Periodic Expert Checks
Lastly, while personal care goes a long way, nothing beats the trained eye of a professional. Regular expert inspections can unearth underlying issues or potential future problems, ensuring your engine stays ahead of the curve.

In the grand orchestra of car maintenance, the engine plays the lead role. Its care is not just about periodic checks but also about understanding, love, and respect. By adhering to these ten commandments of engine care, we don't just ensure a vehicle that runs; we guarantee a car that sings, dances, and celebrates every journey with us. Here's to the many more miles of harmonious drives ahead!

Chapter 4: Navigating the Electrical Maze

Overview of the Automotive Electrical System

Cars are a beautiful blend of raw power and finesse. The sturdy, rhythmic thud of the engine is married harmoniously to the delicate dance of electrical impulses. It's this dance that breathes life into a vehicle, making it more than just an assembly of metal and rubber. The electrical system, the car's nervous system, brings forth a symphony of sights and sounds, from the soothing hum of the radio to the beckoning glow of dashboard lights.

The Heartbeat of Electrons: Beginning at the Battery

Every pulse, every spark begins its journey at the car's battery. Think of this rectangular marvel as a reservoir, holding onto an immense amount of electrical energy, waiting for the right moment to release it. The moment you turn the ignition key, the battery springs into action, sending a torrent of electricity to the starter motor, bringing the engine to life. Yet, the battery's role doesn't end here. As you cruise down the road, it continues to play the role of a guardian, stabilizing the voltage and ensuring every component gets its required dose of electricity.

The Symphony's Conductor: The Alternator

With the engine now alive and roaring, the alternator takes the stage. As you accelerate, the alternator transforms mechanical energy into electrical energy, ensuring that the battery remains charged and the car's electrical needs are met. It's a tireless performer, orchestrating the flow of electricity, ensuring that neither a surplus nor a deficit disrupts the vehicle's harmony.

Lights, Sounds, Action: The Fuses and Relays

In this vast electrical landscape, protection is paramount. Enter the fuses and relays. These small components act as gatekeepers. Fuses ensure that no component draws more electricity than it should, protecting the system from potential damage. On the other hand, relays act as switches, controlling the flow of electricity to larger components, ensuring they operate seamlessly.

The Art of Communication: Sensors and Computers

Modern cars are intelligent beings. They observe, learn, and react, thanks to a plethora of sensors and onboard computers. Sensors, scattered across the vehicle, act as the car's eyes and ears. They monitor everything: from engine temperature to oxygen levels in the exhaust. These readings are then fed to the onboard computers, which process this information and make split-second decisions, optimizing performance, safety, and efficiency. It's a continuous conversation, one that ensures your journey is smooth and enjoyable.

Entertainment and Beyond: Infotainment Systems

No journey is complete without a song or two. Modern infotainment systems, with their touchscreens and voice commands, are a testament to the marvels of automotive electronics. They are more than just a radio or a navigation tool. They connect us to the world, play our favorite tunes, guide us to our destination, and sometimes even read our messages aloud. It's the car's way of ensuring that while it takes care of the road, you can enjoy the moments.

The Shield of Safety: Electronic Safety Systems

While enjoying the moments, safety is paramount. Modern vehicles come equipped with a suite of electronic safety systems. Anti-lock brakes that prevent skidding, electronic stability control that keeps the car on its intended path, and airbag systems that deploy in the blink of an eye, are all orchestrated by the car's electrical system. These systems continuously monitor the vehicle's status, ready to leap into action when needed, ensuring that every journey is not just enjoyable but safe.

The Future Beckons: Electric and Hybrid Vehicles

As we stand at the crossroads of automotive evolution, the role of the electrical system becomes even more pronounced. With the rise of electric and hybrid vehicles, the once auxiliary electrical system now takes center stage, powering the vehicle, ensuring it meets the demands of the modern world while treading gently on our planet.

Starting System

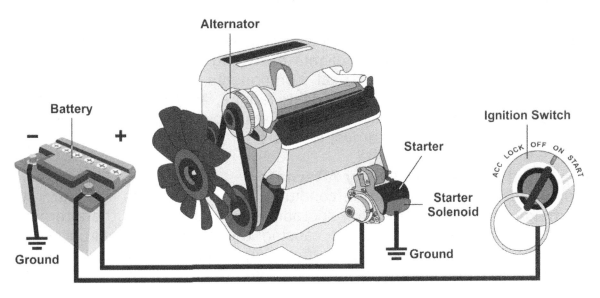

Alternator

Battery

Ground

Starter

Starter
Solenoid

Ground

Ignition Switch

ACC LOCK OFF ON START

Common Electrical Problems and Their Signs

One of the most common electrical conundrums in a vehicle is a weakening battery. If you notice your headlights becoming dimmer, especially when you're operating other electrical components like the radio or air conditioning, it's the battery signaling its fatigue. Another telltale sign is the engine cranking slower than usual during startups. A fading battery doesn't just need a recharge; sometimes, it's a cry for replacement.

The Silent Symphony: Faulty Alternator
Your battery might be in prime condition, but if your car's lights are still dimming or you're experiencing sporadic electrical failures, the alternator might be the unseen conductor causing the discord. A malfunctioning alternator can't charge the battery effectively. If you've ever seen a battery warning light illuminating your dashboard or experienced a car stalling for no apparent reason, it's the alternator waving a red flag.

The Unresponsive Entertainer: Infotainment System Glitches
In today's digitized era, the infotainment system is the heart of in-car entertainment and navigation. However, like any tech marvel, it isn't devoid of glitches. If the system freezes often, fails to connect to your devices, or randomly restarts, it's more than just a minor software hiccup; the car's electrical system might be sending distress signals.

The Inexplicable Behavior: Electrical Shorts
Ever faced a situation where operating one component, say the turn signal, results in the activation of another, like the windshield wipers? These seemingly random occurrences are due to electrical shorts, where wires, stripped of their insulating sheaths, touch each other or the car's metal body. It's not just an amusing quirk; it's a sign that your vehicle's electrical maze has a mischievous gremlin that needs addressing.

The Silent Alarm: Non-functioning Safety Features
The real gravity of electrical issues shines through when the guardians of your safety, like the airbags or anti-lock brakes, become unresponsive. Warning lights related to these systems aren't just indicators; they're loud clarions alerting you to potential dangers lurking in your car's electrical circuits.

A Sudden Darkness: Failing Fuses

Fuses are the unsung heroes, the silent protectors of the electrical realm. When they detect an overload, they sacrifice themselves to save the system. So, if a component—be it your car's radio, lights, or fans—suddenly stops working, it could be a blown fuse raising its hand, signaling its noble demise.

The Ghost in the Machine: Random Error Messages

Modern cars, with their array of sensors, often display error messages on dashboards to inform drivers of potential issues. But if you're bombarded with random, inconsistent warnings, it's not a sign of multiple failures; it might be an electrical glitch causing these phantom alarms.

Troubleshooting Techniques

For many, the car's electrical system feels like an intricate dance of electrons, a web of connections that's as bewildering as it is essential. However, with a keen sense of observation and a touch of patience, you can troubleshoot some of these electrical enigmas without becoming a certified mechanic. Let's journey together through this electrical odyssey.

A Tale of Two Tests: Battery and Alternator

Eyes on the Dashboard: The first indication of a potential electrical issue often comes from the dashboard. Lights refusing to turn off or a lit battery icon might suggest problems with either the battery or the alternator.

The Headlight Test: Turn on your vehicle's headlights before starting the engine. If they are dim and brighten once the engine is running, it's an indication that the battery's charge is weak and it might be on its last legs.

The Rev Test: With the engine running, get a friend to observe the brightness of the headlights. If they get brighter as you rev the engine and dim as you let it idle, the alternator might be the culprit.

The Curious Case of Failing Fuses

Visual Inspection: The simplest way to identify a blown fuse is through a visual check. A melted or broken wire inside the fuse or a scorched appearance usually suggests a fuse has met its end.

Multimeter Magic: Using a multimeter set to continuity, you can check a fuse's health. By touching the multimeter's probes to the fuse's terminals, a good fuse will give a beep or show a zero reading.

Deciphering the Dilemma of Dimming Lights

Battery Health: If lights dim momentarily and return to their normal brightness, it can be a sign of a battery nearing its end. It's wise to test or replace the battery if it's old.

Ground Wire Woes: An unstable connection can also cause fluctuating light intensity. Ensure that the ground wire, which completes the circuit by connecting to the car's body, is secured tightly.

The Radio's Mysterious Rebellion

Antenna Angst: If your car radio receives some stations clearly but distorts others, it might be a misbehaving antenna. Ensure it's fully extended and undamaged.

Speaker Sorrows: Static noises or uneven sound can point towards aging or damaged speakers. Sometimes, simply checking the wire connections can make a world of difference.

The Window's Sluggish Slide
Electric windows moving slower than usual? It might not always be an electrical concern. Sometimes, window channels can become dirty or dry, causing friction. A simple lubrication might solve the riddle.

Intermittent Wiper Woes
If your windshield wipers occasionally act possessed, working sometimes and sulking others, it might be a relay issue. Relays, which are switches controlled by electrical power, often dictate the rhythm of wipers.

Decoding the Dance of Dashboard Lights
Dashboard lights flickering or behaving erratically often point towards a voltage fluctuation. A simple voltage test can highlight whether it's a battery, alternator, or a more complex electrical concern.

When to DIY vs. When to Call an Expert

As we journey through the maze of a vehicle's electrical system, there's a pivotal crossroads that every car owner will encounter: the decision to take matters into their own hands or to delegate to a seasoned professional. It's a delicate balance of confidence, cost, and caution. Let's illuminate this decision-making process.

Harnessing the Power of Observation

Initial Intuition: Before diving deep into repair manuals or online forums, the first step is always self-awareness. Often, your vehicle will communicate with you, be it through a flickering light, an unusual sound, or a peculiar smell. These signs can sometimes indicate the severity of an issue. A minor flicker may fall within the DIY domain, but a burning smell often screams for an expert's intervention.

The Complexity Conundrum

Simple Swaps: Some tasks are straightforward, like replacing a blown fuse, changing a bulb, or even installing a new battery. If you've ventured into minor electrical tasks at home, these should feel like familiar territory.

Wiring Wonders: As the complexity escalates, so should your caution. If an issue involves removing major components or delving deep into the car's wiring system, it's wise to weigh the risks. A misstep can not only intensify the issue but could introduce new problems.

Time: The Silent Decision Maker

Speedy Solutions: DIY often comes with the appeal of immediate results. If you're confident in your abilities and the task at hand is within your skillset, it can be quicker to fix minor issues yourself rather than wait for an appointment with a mechanic.

Intricate Investigations: Complex electrical problems may require hours of diagnostic work. Even if you're handy with tools, it's essential to ask: Do I have the time and patience to diagnose and remedy this issue? If the answer leans towards uncertainty, it's probably best to consult an expert.

Tools and Terrain

Basic Toolbox Triumphs: For many minor electrical tasks, a basic car toolkit, coupled with a multimeter, can suffice. These are tasks where the boundary between DIY and professional help is blurred by simplicity.

Specialist Gear Gaps: Some repairs require specialized tools or diagnostic machines. If an issue demands such equipment, it often makes more financial sense to pay for a professional's time than to invest in tools you'll use once.

Cost Considerations

Immediate vs. Long-Term: While handling minor issues yourself can save immediate out-of-pocket costs, it's essential to factor in the long-term implications. A temporary fix might bring back the issue in a more severe form, leading to heftier bills down the road.

Chapter 5: Cooling System Mastery

Role and Components of the Radiator

At its core, the radiator is a type of heat exchanger designed to transfer thermal energy from one medium to another for the purpose of cooling the engine. Simply put, it keeps your engine from overheating and ensures that it operates at the right temperature, regardless of external conditions.

The Heart of the Radiator: Components that Make the Magic Happen

Core and Cooling Fins: The core is central to the radiator's function. It's filled with a cooling fluid that absorbs the engine's heat. Surrounding this core are cooling fins—a series of thin metal plates—that dissipate the heat into the air as the cooling fluid circulates.

Tanks and Tubes: On either side of the radiator core, you'll find tanks made of plastic or metal. These tanks hold the coolant and are connected by a series of tubes, ensuring the coolant fluid's constant flow.

Pressure Cap: This seemingly inconspicuous component plays a pivotal role. It maintains the coolant's pressure, ensuring the boiling point remains high and the freezing point low. Think of it as a thermostat for the coolant, maintaining a steady temperature.

Outlet and Inlet: These are the entry and exit points for the coolant. The hot coolant from the engine enters the radiator through the inlet, travels through the tubes, loses heat, and exits cooler through the outlet, ready to absorb more heat from the engine.

The Radiator's Symphony: A Dance of Heat Exchange
Imagine you've just completed a marathon. As you rest, your body cools down, readying you for your next adventure. The radiator works similarly for your vehicle.
As your engine works, it produces heat. Left unchecked, this heat can be detrimental, damaging the engine and its components. Here's where the radiator steps in, working diligently to keep everything cool and efficient.

The hot coolant, carrying heat from the engine, flows into the radiator. As it meanders through the tubes, the heat gets transferred to the fins. These fins, in turn, release the heat into the atmosphere. This dance continues, ensuring the engine remains at its optimal temperature.

The Unsung Heroes: Auxiliary Components

Cooling Fans: On a breezy day, you might fan yourself to cool down faster. Similarly, cooling fans kick into action when the air around the radiator isn't enough to dissipate the heat efficiently. These fans ensure that the air circulation remains optimal, especially during idle times or slow traffic.

Thermostat: The thermostat is the unsung hero, controlling the flow of coolant based on the engine's temperature. If the engine's too cold, the thermostat restricts the flow, allowing the engine to warm up. When things get too hot, it opens up, allowing the coolant to do its magic.

Water Pump: The heart of the cooling system, the water pump, ensures that the coolant keeps moving, circulating from the engine to the radiator and back.

Radiator's Role Beyond Cooling

While the primary role of the radiator is to keep the engine cool, its importance stretches beyond that. By maintaining the engine's temperature, it ensures that the engine oil remains at its optimal viscosity, lubricating the engine efficiently. This results in better fuel efficiency, lower emissions, and extends the lifespan of the engine.

Moreover, a well-functioning radiator also ensures that the heater inside your vehicle works efficiently. On a cold day, the heat from the coolant is used to warm the inside of your car, ensuring you remain cozy despite the frigid conditions outside.

Automotive Cooling System

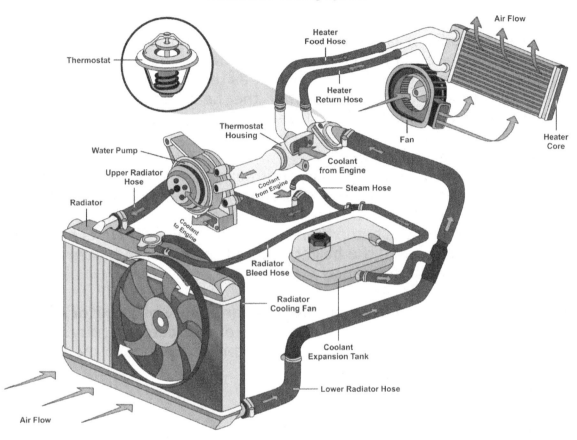

Coolant Level Monitoring and Replacement

Your vehicle's radiator is the mastermind behind ensuring that the engine runs cool. But the coolant it circulates is the actual medium that facilitates this vital cooling process. Think of coolant as the lifeblood of your radiator: it's the messenger that carries away the heat, ensuring your engine functions optimally. Monitoring its level and quality is paramount.

The Basics: What is Coolant?

Coolant, sometimes referred to as antifreeze, is a mixture of water and specific chemicals that circulates through the engine and radiator. Its primary function is to absorb heat from the engine and release it through the radiator. But it doesn't stop there; the coolant also prevents freezing in cold conditions and raises the boiling point of the water in hotter climates, ensuring consistent performance.

Reading Between the Levels: The Why and How of Monitoring

Over time, coolant can get consumed, leak, or degrade in quality. This can lead to reduced efficiency in cooling and potential damage to the vehicle.

The Why:

1. **Protection Against Extremes:** By maintaining the right coolant level, you safeguard the engine against freezing in the cold and overheating in warmer conditions.

2. **Preventing Corrosion:** Modern coolants contain corrosion inhibitors. Keeping the coolant fresh and at the correct level ensures these inhibitors protect the engine and radiator from rust and sediment build-up.

3. **Optimal Lubrication:** The coolant also provides lubrication to the water pump, ensuring its longevity.

The How:

1. **Regular Visual Checks:** Most vehicles come with a transparent coolant reservoir with markings that indicate minimum and maximum

levels. Periodic checks, perhaps during refueling, can provide quick insights into the coolant level.

2. **Feel the Radiator:** Only when the engine is cold, open the radiator cap and look inside. The coolant should be near the brim. If it's much below, it's time for a top-up.

3. **Quality Inspection:** While the level is essential, so is the quality. Over time, coolant can become dirty or discolored. If it looks murky or has particles floating, it might be time for a replacement.

Switching it Up: The Process of Coolant Replacement

Occasional top-ups are a part of regular maintenance, but there will come a time when the coolant needs a complete replacement.

1. **Drain the Old Coolant:** With the engine off and cold, place a container under the radiator and open the drain plug. Allow the old coolant to flow out.

2. **Flush the System:** Using a radiator flush solution or distilled water, fill the radiator. Start the engine with the heater on maximum and let it run for a while. Then, drain the flush solution or water.

3. **Refill with New Coolant:** With the drain plug securely in place, slowly pour the new coolant mixture into the radiator. Once full, replace the cap and run the engine to circulate the new coolant.

4. **Check for Leaks:** After the replacement, it's a good idea to inspect for any leaks or loose hoses. Ensuring everything's secure will prevent future coolant losses.

Treading with Caution: Safety First

While coolant plays a crucial role in your vehicle's health, it can be hazardous to humans and pets. It often has a sweet smell that might be attractive to animals, but ingestion can be deadly. Always store coolant in sealed containers, out of reach of children and pets. If you're replacing the coolant yourself, ensure you dispose of the old coolant responsibly, adhering to local regulations.

Tips and Tricks for Efficient Cooling

Before diving into tips, it's essential to grasp the broader picture. Your vehicle's cooling system isn't just about the radiator and the coolant; it's a symphony of parts working in harmony. From the water pump circulating coolant, the thermostat controlling temperature, to the fans and belts ensuring everything moves as it should - every piece has its part to play.

The Thermostat: Guardian of Temperature
An unsung hero of the cooling system is the humble thermostat. It determines when to allow coolant to flow through the engine. When the engine's cold, it restricts flow, helping the engine warm up quickly. When the engine's hot, it opens up, letting coolant flow to dissipate heat.

Tip: If your vehicle seems to be running hotter than usual, or if the temperature isn't rising at all, your thermostat might be acting up. It's a relatively inexpensive part, but its proper functioning is crucial. Check and replace if necessary.

The Water Pump: The Heartbeat of Cooling
The water pump, driven by the engine, circulates coolant throughout the system.

Trick: A telltale sign of a failing water pump is a coolant leak at the front-center of your car. If you hear a whining sound coming from the front of your engine, combined with a coolant leak, it's time to inspect the water pump.

Hoses and Belts: The Vessels and Muscles
Just as our body has veins and muscles, your car's cooling system has hoses and belts. The hoses circulate coolant; the belts drive parts like the water pump and fans.

Tip: Every now and then, give these a visual inspection. Look for cracks, bulges, or leaks in hoses and check belts for signs of wear or fraying. Replacing them preemptively can save a roadside breakdown.

Keeping it Clean: Radiator Maintenance
Your radiator thrives on cleanliness. Both its interior and exterior need to be free from obstructions.

Tip: Ensure the exterior of the radiator is free from debris like leaves or plastic bags. These can prevent airflow, reducing cooling efficiency. Additionally, an occasional radiator flush removes sediment and corrosion from its interior, ensuring optimal performance.

Fan Efficiency: Ensuring Airflow
While driving at speed, the natural airflow cools the radiator. But when idling or driving slowly, the cooling fans take over.

Trick: If your car tends to overheat in traffic but cools down at speed, your fans might be the culprits. Check for their proper operation. Also, modern cars often have electric fans that turn on based on coolant temperature; ensure their sensors work correctly.

Watch the Gauges: They Communicate
Your dashboard isn't there just for speed and fuel levels. The temperature gauge provides crucial feedback.

Tip: Get familiar with where the needle usually sits. If it starts deviating frequently towards the hotter end, it's signaling a potential issue. Don't ignore it; overheating can lead to significant engine damage.

Seasonal Care: Summer vs. Winter
Different seasons pose different challenges for the cooling system.

Trick for Summer: Ensure your coolant is topped up, and its mixture is suitable for high temperatures. Check the functioning of your cooling fans, as they'll work overtime during summer stop-and-go traffic.

Trick for Winter: Ensure the coolant mixture is appropriate for freezing temperatures. A higher concentration of antifreeze can prevent the coolant from freezing and cracking the engine block.

Chapter 6: A Breath of Fresh Air: The A/C System

Basic Principles and Components

A vehicle's A/C isn't as simple as pumping out cool or hot air. It's a carefully orchestrated symphony of components working together to maintain a comfortable environment inside your car. Just as a conductor guides each instrument in an orchestra to create a melodious tune, each part of the A/C system plays its role to ensure you remain comfortable, regardless of the conditions outside.

Cooling: More Than Just Cold Air

The primary purpose of the A/C system isn't merely to provide cold air. It's to regulate the temperature, ensuring the environment inside the car is tailored to your liking.

The heart of this operation is the **compressor**. Think of it as the maestro of the A/C orchestra. Powered by the engine, it compresses the refrigerant, turning it from a low-pressure gas to a high-pressure one. This is the first step in the cooling process, with the refrigerant now prepared to absorb heat.

Now enters the **condenser**. As you drive, air flows through the front grille, passing through the condenser. Here, the high-pressure refrigerant releases the heat it has absorbed, cooling it down as it turns into a liquid form.

Yet, our journey of cooling is not over. The liquid refrigerant makes its way to the **expansion valve**. This little component reduces the pressure of the refrigerant, turning it back into a gas and further cooling it down.

This super-cool refrigerant then travels through the **evaporator**, which is located inside the cabin of your vehicle. As the cabin's warm air is pulled over the evaporator, the refrigerant absorbs this heat. The blower fan then pushes this now cool air into the cabin, much to your relief.

Heating: Your Winter Saviour

The A/C system isn't just for those scorching summer days. When winter comes knocking with its icy fingers, your car's heating system becomes your best friend.

The heater doesn't need refrigerant. Instead, it takes advantage of the heat your engine produces. The **heater core**, a small radiator-like component, uses hot coolant from the engine. As the blower fan pushes cabin air over the heater core, this heat is transferred to the air, warming it up before it wafts into the cabin.

Humidity and Ventilation: The Unsung Heroes
Cooling and heating might be the stars of the show, but humidity control and ventilation play their crucial roles too. Ever noticed your windows fogging up? That's due to moisture. The A/C system also acts as a dehumidifier. As air passes over the cold evaporator, moisture condenses, effectively removing it from the cabin air.
Ventilation ensures a continuous supply of fresh air, replacing stale air and preventing odors. Fresh air, sourced from outside, is filtered to remove pollutants, ensuring you're always breathing clean, crisp air.

Modern Marvels: Automatic Climate Control
Gone are the days of fiddling with dials to get the temperature just right. Modern vehicles come equipped with automatic climate control systems. You set your desired temperature, and the system takes care of the rest, adjusting fan speeds, choosing between heating and cooling, and ensuring the cabin remains at your preferred comfort level.

Troubleshooting A/C Malfunctions

It's a sunny day, the kind where sunglasses seem inadequate, and you're ready to drive off to your next adventure. As you slide into the car, you eagerly turn on the A/C, awaiting that familiar cool embrace. Instead, you're greeted with a faint gust of warm air or, worse, an odd smell. Panic sets in. What's going wrong? Before you spiral into dismay, let's delve into common A/C malfunctions and how you can play detective to identify them.

The Cold Shoulder: A Lack of Cool Air

Perhaps the most disheartening A/C malfunction is when it fails to produce cold air on a day you need it most. Several culprits could be responsible:

- **Refrigerant Leaks**: This is the lifeblood of your A/C system, and without it, the system cannot cool the air. If there's a noticeable lack of cool air, it's possible there's a leak somewhere in the system. Traces of oil around A/C components or hissing sounds can sometimes hint at this issue.

- **Failed Compressor**: Remember the maestro of our A/C orchestra? If the compressor isn't working, the entire system struggles. A frequent cause could be a broken or worn-out belt.

- **Clogged Expansion Valve**: If this valve is blocked, the refrigerant can't flow into the evaporator, hampering the cooling process.

Odoriferous Offenses: Unpleasant Smells

A functional A/C should make your journey comfortable, not assault your nostrils. If there's a peculiar scent wafting from the vents:

- **Mold and Mildew**: Over time, especially in humid conditions, moisture can accumulate in the A/C system, allowing mold and mildew to grow. This growth often produces a musty odor.

- **Old Filters**: Air filters, if not replaced regularly, can become clogged with dirt, dust, and other contaminants. This not only restricts airflow but can also produce a stale smell.

Weak Winds: Reduced Airflow

Your A/C is producing cold air, but it feels like it's being delivered with the enthusiasm of a tired sigh. This reduced airflow can detract from your driving comfort.

- **Blower Motor Issues**: This component is responsible for pushing air through the vents. If it's malfunctioning or the associated resistor is damaged, airflow can be severely hampered.

- **Blocked Vents**: Over time, debris can accumulate in the air ducts, restricting the flow of air.

Sounding Off: Unusual Noises

Your A/C should operate with a gentle hum, not a cacophony of strange sounds. If you're hearing unusual noises when the A/C is on:

- **Loose Hardware**: Sometimes, the solution is as simple as tightening a bolt or screw. Loose components can rattle or create vibrations.

- **Damaged Compressor**: If the compressor is failing, it can sometimes produce a grinding or squealing noise. Don't ignore this; the compressor is vital to the A/C system.

Foggy Affairs: Windows Misting Up

If your windows fog up when you turn on the A/C, especially in cold weather:

- **Poor Dehumidification**: The A/C system doubles as a dehumidifier. If it's not doing its job efficiently, moisture can accumulate, causing windows to mist.

- **Heater Core Issues**: Remember our winter savior? If the heater core is leaking or malfunctioning, it can cause misting on the interior windows.

DIY Repairs and Maintenance Tips

Imagine this: The sun blazes outside, and as you enter your car, you're enveloped in a serene coolness, knowing that you played an active part in ensuring this comfort. The sense of accomplishment from handling minor A/C issues yourself is rewarding, both for your self-confidence and your wallet. With a little knowledge, patience, and the right tools, you can keep your A/C system running smoothly. Let's dive into the realm of DIY and unveil some secrets to A/C system maintenance.

Refreshing the Filters

Starting Small with Big Impact: One of the most straightforward tasks in A/C maintenance is changing the air filter. A clogged filter not only restricts airflow but also forces the system to work harder, leading to more wear and tear.

How to Do It: Locate the cabin air filter (often behind the glove compartment or under the dashboard). After removing it, simply replace it with a new one. It's a good practice to change the filter every 12,000 to 15,000 miles or at least once a year, but refer to your vehicle's manual for specific recommendations.

The Right Amount: Topping Up the Refrigerant

Keeping Cool with Chemistry: The refrigerant is the essence of your A/C system, absorbing and releasing heat to keep the air cool. Over time, the refrigerant level can drop, affecting the system's efficiency.

How to Do It: Purchase a refrigerant kit from an auto parts store. After locating the low-side service port (typically on the larger A/C line), connect the refrigerant can and gauge. Add the refrigerant slowly, monitoring the gauge and ensuring not to overfill. Remember, safety first! Always wear protective gloves and eyewear.

Cleaning the Condenser

Unclogging the Heart: The condenser plays a pivotal role in dissipating the heat absorbed by the refrigerant.

Over time, it can become clogged with dirt, leaves, and other debris, hampering its efficiency.

How to Do It: First, locate the condenser (usually at the front of the car, behind the grille). Using a gentle brush, remove any loose debris. Then, with a garden hose, spray it down from the top, moving vertically to help push the debris out. Avoid high-pressure washers, as they can damage the delicate fins of the condenser.

Evaporator Maintenance

Clearing the Chill Chamber: The evaporator's role is to absorb heat from the car's interior, but its moist environment makes it a magnet for mold and mildew.

How to Do It: Accessing the evaporator can be tricky, often requiring the removal of the dashboard. For those not ready to tackle this, a simpler approach is using an evaporator cleaner. Spray it into the exterior air intake vents (located at the base of the windshield) while the A/C is running, letting it circulate and clean the system.

Checking the Belts

The Lifelines of Movement: The serpentine belt powers the A/C compressor. If it's worn or loose, the compressor can't function optimally.
How to Do It: Visually inspect the belt for signs of wear, like cracks or fraying. If it seems loose, you might need to adjust the tension or replace the belt. For many, this can be a more advanced DIY task, so if you're not comfortable, seek assistance.

The Importance of A/C Health

The Air Conditioning (A/C) system, while often taken for granted, serves as a quiet companion in our journeys, ensuring our comfort irrespective of the world outside. Beyond just comfort, though, a well-maintained A/C system has deeper implications for both the driver and the car.

A Sanctuary of Well-being

Breathing Quality Air: The air we breathe significantly affects our health. A functional A/C system ensures that the air circulated within the vehicle is clean, free of pollutants, allergens, and even harmful microorganisms. Especially in urban settings with higher pollution levels, a car can act as a haven of clean air, but only if its A/C system is in top shape.

Stress and Mood Enhancer: Think about the last time you drove in extreme temperatures. The discomfort can be a significant distraction, leading to stress, agitation, and reduced cognitive abilities. A well-functioning A/C contributes to a calm, focused mindset, which is vital for safe driving.

Shielding Your Car's Integrity

Moisture Control: One of the unsung roles of the A/C is controlling humidity levels inside the vehicle. Excess moisture can fog up windows, impairing vision. Over time, it can also seep into the car's interior, leading to mold, rust, and deterioration. By maintaining a dry environment, the A/C system indirectly contributes to road safety and the longevity of your vehicle.

Resale Value: Like all aspects of car maintenance, a well-functioning A/C system boosts the vehicle's resale value. Prospective buyers often check the A/C's performance as an indicator of overall vehicle care.

The Symphony of Performance and Efficiency

Optimizing Fuel Consumption: A compromised A/C system has to work harder, putting additional strain on the engine and, consequently, consuming more fuel.

While the difference might not be glaringly obvious in the short term, over extended periods, a healthy A/C can contribute to noticeable fuel savings.

Preventing Domino Failures: Car systems are intricately linked. An issue with the A/C can lead to problems elsewhere, such as undue strain on the car battery or alternator. By ensuring your A/C's health, you're indirectly ensuring the health of various other components.

The Whispers of Nature

Environmental Responsibility: Leaking refrigerant from A/C systems can be harmful to the environment. Modern vehicles use refrigerants that have a lower environmental impact, but leaks can still contribute to greenhouse gas emissions. Regular maintenance can help spot and rectify these issues, making your drive a tad greener.

Chapter 7: Stopping Power: The Braking System

Operational Mechanics of Brakes

Every time we press the brake pedal, a beautifully orchestrated series of events unfolds. The brake system isn't just about halting the car; it's about controlling its speed and ensuring a smooth and safe deceleration.

Beneath the Pedal's Pressure

A World of Fluid Dynamics: When you apply pressure to the brake pedal, that force is transferred to the brake fluid contained within the brake lines. This fluid, in its sealed environment, acts as a medium to carry your foot's force to the brake components at the wheels.

Master Cylinder – The Master's Baton: The master cylinder is the heart of the brake fluid system. It contains reservoirs for brake fluid and ensures that the fluid remains under pressure. Think of it as the conductor of an orchestra, ensuring every instrument (or brake component) plays its part perfectly.

From Force to Friction: The brake fluid, now under pressure, travels to the brake calipers (for disc brakes) or brake cylinders (for drum brakes). These components push the brake pads or shoes against the rotating parts of the wheel, the discs or drums. This application creates friction, which in turn slows down or stops the wheel.

Disc vs. Drum – The Duet of Braking

While both disc and drum brakes rely on the same principle of using friction to halt motion, their design and operation vary.

Disc Brakes – The Dynamic Dancer: Predominantly found on the front wheels of modern vehicles, disc brakes consist of a rotor (a flat, round piece of metal) that spins with the wheel. When the brakes are applied, calipers squeeze brake pads against this rotor. This action generates friction, slowing the wheel down.

Drum Brakes – The Resonant Rhythms: Often found on the rear wheels of many vehicles, drum brakes have a rounded drum that rotates along with the wheel. Inside this drum are brake shoes. When the brakes are applied, these shoes press outwards against the drum's inner surface. Again, friction plays its part, causing the wheel to slow or stop.

The Balancing Act

Anti-lock Braking System (ABS) – Grace under Pressure: ABS is a modern marvel that prevents wheels from locking up during intense braking. If wheels lock up, especially on slippery surfaces, vehicles can skid uncontrollably. ABS uses sensors to detect wheel speed. If one or more wheels are about to lock, the system modulates brake pressure, ensuring traction and control.

Distributing the Force – Proportional Symphony: Not every wheel needs the same amount of braking force. Factors like vehicle weight distribution, road conditions, and vehicle speed play a part. The brake force proportioning system ensures that the right amount of force is distributed between the front and rear brakes.

Brake Pads and Shoes – The Unsung Heroes
These components bear the brunt of the friction and heat generated during braking. They're made of materials specifically designed to handle these stresses while providing consistent braking performance.

With friction comes heat, and managing this heat is crucial. Disc brakes, due to their open design, dissipate heat more efficiently. Some high-performance vehicles even have ventilated rotors, further aiding in cooling. Drum brakes, being enclosed, have a harder time dissipating heat, which can sometimes affect performance during prolonged braking.

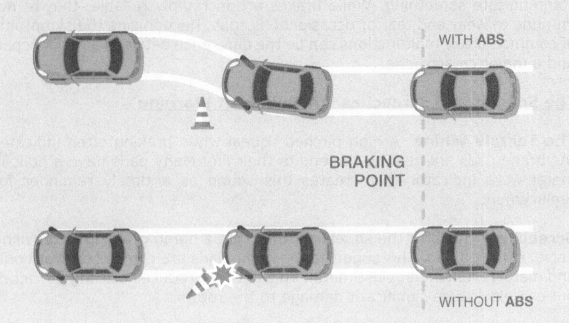

THE ADVANTAGES OF AN
ANTI-LOCK BRAKING SYSTEM

WITH **ABS**

BRAKING
POINT

WITHOUT **ABS**

Common Brake Malfunctions and Symptoms

Just like how a good friend can sense when you're not feeling your best, so too can an attentive driver discern when their car's brakes are trying to communicate something. While brakes are incredibly reliable, they're not immune to wear and tear or occasional hiccups. Recognizing the symptoms of common brake malfunctions can be the difference between a minor repair and a major catastrophe.

The Squeals and Screeches – A Melody of Warning

The Telltale Whine: A high-pitched squeal when braking often indicates the brake pads are nearing the end of their life. Many pads have a built-in metal wear indicator that creates this sound as a timely reminder for replacement.

Screeching Halts: If the squealing turns into a harsh grinding or growling noise, it's a red flag. This suggests the brake pads are completely worn out, and metal is rubbing against metal. This not only reduces braking efficiency but can also cause significant damage to the rotors.

The Vibrations and Pulses – A Dance of Discomfort

Rhythmic Pulsing: If you feel a pulsing or throbbing in the brake pedal or steering wheel when braking, it often points to a warped rotor. Rotors can warp from excessive heat or uneven wear, affecting the smooth operation of the brakes.

Shaky Stops: If the entire vehicle shudders when brakes are applied, it might hint at issues with the brake drums or rotors. Such vibrations compromise the effectiveness of the braking system.

The Mushy or Hard Pedal – Sensing the Pressure

Going to the Floor: A brake pedal that feels unusually soft or goes all the way to the floor indicates a potential brake fluid leak or air trapped in the brake lines. This condition severely affects braking power and requires immediate attention.

Stubborn Resistance: Conversely, a brake pedal that's hard to press down might suggest problems with the brake booster or issues within the vacuum system. It increases the effort needed to stop the vehicle and can be exhausting for the driver.

Dragging Sensations – The Invisible Hand

The Unwilling Acceleration: If you feel like you have to give more gas than usual to move the car or if it seems like something is holding it back, a brake caliper or brake shoes might be sticking. Not only does this reduce fuel efficiency, but it also leads to premature wear of the brake components.

Unusual Responses – The Twists and Turns

The Unintended Swerve: If your vehicle pulls to one side when braking, it could be due to uneven wear of brake pads, a collapsed brake hose, or impurities in the brake fluid. Such behavior can be unpredictable and dangerous, especially in emergency braking situations.

A Noseful of Warning – Odors and Aromas

The Acrid Burn: A sharp, burning smell when driving is never a good sign. When related to brakes, it often indicates overheated brake pads or shoes creating excessive friction. This condition can lead to brake fade, reducing braking efficiency when it's needed the most.

Maintenance and Upgrades

The braking system is, without a doubt, one of the most critical safety features of any vehicle. Every twist, turn, and unexpected stop relies on the precise function of this system. However, like any other part of your car, the brakes require regular attention, care, and sometimes, an upgrade. Let's navigate the road of maintaining and upgrading your vehicle's brakes to ensure that every journey is not only smooth but also safe.

The Gentle Art of Brake Maintenance

Fluid Dynamics: Brake fluid plays an indispensable role in transmitting the force from your foot on the pedal to the brakes on the wheels. Over time, brake fluid can absorb moisture, reducing its effectiveness and leading to corrosion in the brake system. For this reason, it's recommended to replace the brake fluid every two years or as per your vehicle manufacturer's guidelines.

Brake Pads - Keeping the Friction in Check: Brake pads bear the brunt of the braking system's work. Depending on driving habits and conditions, the lifespan of brake pads can vary. It's wise to have them inspected during routine maintenance checks. Waiting too long can lead to reduced braking performance and even damage to other brake components.

Rotors - The Smooth Operators: Brake rotors, or discs, should exhibit a smooth, clean surface. Any grooves, cracks, or warping can reduce the efficiency of the braking system. While rotors can be resurfaced or "turned" to extend their life, there comes a point when replacement is the best option.

Hoses & Lines - The Silent Carriers: These components transport brake fluid from the master cylinder to the brakes. They should be inspected regularly for signs of wear, cracking, or leaks. Given their role in maintaining the pressure required for braking, any compromise can lead to a catastrophic failure.

Bringing in the New – The World of Brake Upgrades

Sometimes, the standard brakes that come with your vehicle might not be up to par with your needs, especially if you've made modifications to your vehicle or if you engage in activities like towing or racing. Here's where upgrades enter the scene.

Performance Pads – The Next Level of Stopping: Upgrading to performance brake pads can offer enhanced stopping power, reduced brake dust, and even longer life than traditional pads. These pads are designed for specific scenarios, such as high-performance driving or heavy-duty towing.

Disc Upgrades - More than Just a Pretty Face: Performance rotors often feature designs like slots or drilled holes. While they certainly look sporty, these designs also serve practical purposes. They can help dissipate heat more effectively and keep the brake pads clean, offering more consistent braking.

Bigger Calipers - The Bigger, the Better?: Upgrading to larger brake calipers can offer more clamping force, translating to improved stopping power. However, this often requires larger wheels to accommodate the increased size.

Braided Brake Lines – Strength and Precision: Upgrading to braided stainless steel brake lines can provide a firmer pedal feel and increased resistance to damage or wear, especially in challenging driving conditions.

Maintenance of the braking system is not merely a routine; it's an investment in safety and longevity. While regular check-ups and timely replacements are essential, upgrades can offer that extra edge in performance and reliability.

Chapter 8: The Breath of Your Car: Exhaust System

Causes and Signs of Exhaust Issues

A well-functioning exhaust system operates like an orchestra in perfect harmony. As the combustion process unfolds, gases are produced. These gases, potentially harmful to both passengers and the environment, need to be directed away from the car's interior, filtered, and then safely released. This orchestrated process ensures that your car performs optimally, and pollutants are minimized.

However, when something is amiss, this harmonious symphony is disrupted, and the car starts to whisper its woes.

The Culprits Behind Exhaust Disruptions

Age and Wear: Like everything in life, the exhaust system isn't immune to the relentless march of time. As months turn into years, continuous exposure to road conditions, moisture, and the rigors of driving can lead to natural wear and tear.

Physical Damage: Our roads are not always smooth sailing. Potholes, rough terrains, or even minor accidents can result in physical harm to the exhaust system. Sometimes, this damage is immediately apparent, while at other times, the symptoms manifest slowly.

Corrosion: The exhaust is constantly exposed to a combination of high temperatures, moisture, and chemicals. Over time, this mix can become the perfect recipe for corrosion, particularly in areas with salted roads or coastal regions.

Listening to the Signs: Symptoms of an Ailing Exhaust

Sounds and Echoes: One of the first signs of exhaust troubles is often heard rather than seen. A rumbling or hissing noise is not just the car being vocal – it's a cry for help, indicating potential holes or cracks in the exhaust system.

Reduced Fuel Efficiency: Your vehicle suddenly guzzling more fuel than usual? It could be your exhaust system hinting at a problem. A malfunctioning exhaust can negatively impact the engine's performance, leading to increased fuel consumption.

Vibrations: Feeling unexpected vibrations through the steering wheel or foot pedal? It might seem like a minor inconvenience, but it's a sign that something's amiss. These vibrations can be the exhaust's way of saying it's compromised and affecting the car's overall performance.

The Smell of Trouble: The scent of something rotten or the sting of a burning sensation in your nostrils while driving isn't just uncomfortable; it's alarming. These odors can indicate that the exhaust is leaking harmful gases, posing a threat to passengers.

Visual Clues: Sometimes, the story of the exhaust's health is laid out right before our eyes. Rust, holes, or even hanging components are glaring visual cues that the exhaust system needs attention.

Environmental and Health Impacts

Exhaust problems don't just stop at the vehicle; they ripple out, affecting the world around us. A faulty exhaust releases a higher amount of pollutants, contributing to environmental degradation and public health issues. From smog to respiratory problems, the implications of neglecting a malfunctioning exhaust system can be profound.

An Invitation to Intervene

A car's exhaust system, much like the human respiratory system, is vital for its health and performance. Recognizing the signs of exhaust issues is the first step in a dance of proactive intervention. It's an invitation to take action, ensuring that the whispers of our vehicles don't turn into alarming cries for help.

Practical Solutions and Repair Techniques

Just as a skilled doctor listens, analyzes, and then prescribes, tending to an exhaust system requires a careful blend of observation and action. By now, we're attuned to the various whispers and shouts our car may make when the exhaust system is amiss. In this segment, we transition from passive observers to active car caregivers, delving into the practical solutions and repair techniques to bring our exhaust system back to optimal health.

Before diving headfirst into repairs, a precise diagnosis is key. We wouldn't want to change our car's entire exhaust system when all it needed was a simple sealant or patch. Utilize the signs we've discussed: the sounds, the vibrations, and the visual cues. These are our first diagnostic tools. However, for a more comprehensive assessment, considering a professional opinion can often save time and resources in the long run.

Tending to Minor Leaks and Cracks

Sealants and Patches: The market offers various exhaust repair kits that include sealants and patches. These are ideal for minor leaks or small cracks. Applying a sealant or patch is relatively straightforward:

1. Clean the affected area thoroughly, ensuring it's free from dirt or rust.

2. Apply the sealant or adhere the patch as per the product's instructions.

3. Allow it ample time to set.

Remember, these solutions are often temporary. If the problem persists or worsens, it might be time for a more robust intervention.

Addressing Corrosion and Rust

Anti-Corrosion Sprays: For areas showing early signs of rust, anti-corrosion sprays can be a savior. After cleaning the affected area, a quick spray can provide a protective layer, preventing further rusting.

Physical Removal: For more advanced rust spots, consider using a wire brush or sandpaper to scrub away the corrosion. Once removed, applying a protective spray or paint can prevent future occurrences.

Handling Damaged Components

Clamps and Brackets: If a section of the exhaust is sagging or seems loose, it might be due to a failing clamp or bracket. Replacing these is often simple and can be done with basic tools.

Pipe and Muffler Replacement: For more extensive damage, such as large holes or severe corrosion, replacing the affected section might be the best course of action. While this can be done at home with the right tools and a bit of know-how, seeking professional help ensures the job is done right and safely.

When the Problem is Internal
Sometimes, the issue isn't external. Internal components, like the catalytic converter, can become clogged or damaged over time. If your vehicle isn't running efficiently, or you notice unusual smells, this could be the culprit. Replacing a catalytic converter is a task usually best left to professionals, given its integral role in filtering harmful pollutants.

Safety First, Always
While DIY solutions can be gratifying and cost-effective, safety should never be compromised. Always ensure:

- The vehicle is securely raised if you need to work underneath.

- You're equipped with the right safety gear – gloves, goggles, and protective clothing.

- You're working in a well-ventilated area, especially when dealing with chemicals or fumes.

Harnessing Professional Wisdom
There's no shame in seeking professional assistance when things seem out of depth. Mechanics have the tools, expertise, and experience to diagnose and rectify exhaust problems swiftly.

Understanding and Maintaining Key Components

The Harmonious Players of the Exhaust System

Manifold: Our journey starts right at the engine. The manifold collects exhaust gases from the engine's cylinders. It's the gathering point, the stage where all the actors come together before the performance begins. Made typically of cast iron or stainless steel, the manifold should be regularly inspected for cracks or leaks. This ensures that the exhaust gases are directed appropriately down the line.

Oxygen Sensors: Acting as vigilant watchdogs, these sensors monitor the oxygen levels in the exhaust gases. They relay this information to the car's computer, ensuring optimal air-fuel mixture for efficient combustion. Like a fine-tuned ear to music, these sensors need to be sensitive and accurate. Regular checks can ensure they're in top shape, preventing potential mileage and emission issues.

Catalytic Converter: If there were an unsung hero in our car's underbelly, this would be it. The catalytic converter transforms harmful pollutants into less detrimental gases before they exit the tailpipe. Ensuring this component functions effectively is not just about vehicle performance; it's our nod to environmental responsibility. Clogged or damaged converters should be addressed promptly. And remember, due to the precious metals inside, they can be a target for thieves; consider anti-theft measures if necessary.

Muffler: The car's maestro! The muffler's job is to reduce the noise produced by the exhaust. Inside this component, there are chambers and tubes that deflect and redirect sound waves, causing them to cancel each other out. Over time, the muffler can corrode or develop holes, leading to a louder exhaust. Regular inspections can help ensure a quieter, more pleasant drive.

Tailpipe: This is the grand finale, where all the transformed gases make their exit. It's the endpoint of our exhaust system journey. While it might seem like just a simple exit tube, ensuring it's clear and undamaged is crucial for safe and efficient emission of exhaust gases.

The Key to Longevity: Regular Maintenance

Just knowing these components isn't enough. Treating them with care and regular checks ensures the longevity of the entire system. Here are some maintenance tips:

1. **Regular Cleaning**: Just like a musical instrument sounds better when it's clean, our exhaust system performs better when it's free from grime and debris. Regular cleaning, especially of the tailpipe, can prevent build-up that might hinder performance.

2. **Anti-Rust Treatments**: Rust is the nemesis of the exhaust system. Given its location, it's constantly exposed to water, mud, and other corrosive elements. Using anti-rust treatments or sprays can add a protective layer, fending off premature wear.

3. **Prompt Repairs**: Addressing issues when they're minor can prevent more significant, costlier problems down the road. Whether it's a small leak, a rust spot, or a malfunctioning oxygen sensor, timely interventions are key.

4. **Professional Inspections**: Consider periodic inspections by professionals. They have the equipment and expertise to spot potential issues that might be easily missed by the untrained eye.

Our exhaust system is more than just a series of tubes and components. It's a testament to human ingenuity, a bridge between performance and environmental responsibility. By understanding its key players and ensuring they're well-maintained, we not only ensure a smoother drive but also play our part in reducing pollution. As we wrap up this chapter, let's carry forward this newfound knowledge, ensuring our vehicle's "breath" remains clean, efficient, and harmonious with the world around us.

Chapter 9: Fueling Your Journey

Anatomy of the Traditional Fuel System

Before delving into the minutiae, let's envision the journey of fuel. Picture a droplet of gasoline, starting its life in the fuel tank, making its way through a series of pipes, filters, and pumps, eventually ending its odyssey in the engine, where it combusts to propel your vehicle forward. This adventure is not just a mechanical process; it's a transformative journey, making our trips to work, school, or leisure possible.

Embarking from the Reservoir: The Fuel Tank

The fuel tank, often located at the rear of the vehicle, acts as a reservoir. It holds the gasoline or diesel, waiting for its time to shine. Made of corrosion-resistant materials to withstand the volatile nature of fuel, this is where our droplet's journey begins. Periodic checks for leaks, rust, or damage ensure that the tank continues to function as the starting point of our fuel's voyage.

The Guardians of Clean Fuel: Fuel Filters

As our droplet ventures forth, it encounters the fuel filter, a guardian ensuring that only clean fuel reaches the engine. This component filters out any debris, dirt, or contaminants that might have made their way into the tank. Just as our kidneys filter out impurities from our bloodstream, the fuel filter ensures that the engine receives only the purest fuel. Regular replacement of these filters guarantees optimal engine performance and longevity.

Pushing Forward: The Fuel Pump

Now, our droplet needs some encouragement to continue its journey. Enter the fuel pump. Typically located inside or near the fuel tank, this component pushes the fuel towards the engine. The pump ensures a constant and adequate flow, adapting to the engine's demands. Whether you're cruising down a highway or navigating city streets, the pump modulates the fuel flow accordingly. An erratic engine, difficulties starting the car, or poor fuel efficiency can be indicators that the pump might need attention.

Spray and Combust: Fuel Injectors

Approaching the end of its odyssey, our droplet reaches the fuel injectors.

These are nozzles that spray a mist of fuel into the engine's combustion chamber. The transformation from liquid to mist ensures that the fuel burns more efficiently. Over time, these injectors can become clogged or malfunction, leading to reduced engine performance. Regular cleaning ensures that they continue their essential task without a hiccup.

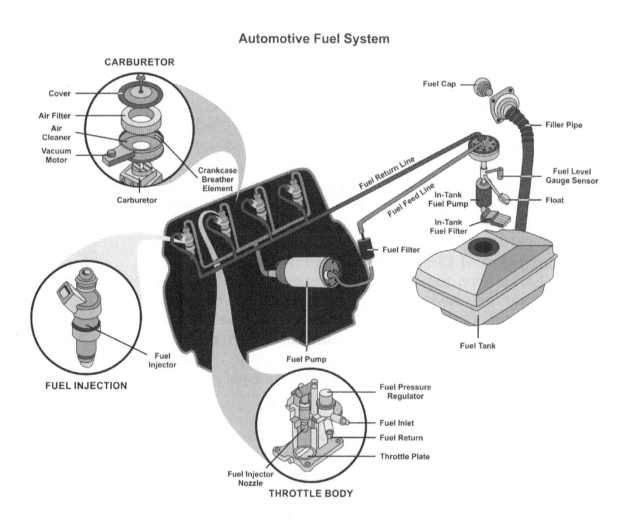

Automotive Fuel System

Delving into Alternative Fuel Options

Gone are the days when gasoline and diesel were the only choices at the pump. As concerns about the environment, economy, and energy security have come to the forefront, the transportation industry has been spurred into an era of innovation. This thirst for progress has given rise to a diverse range of alternative fuels. These are not just conceptual or experimental; many of these options are already powering vehicles on our roads, providing cleaner, more sustainable means of transport.

The Electric Dream: Battery Electric Vehicles (BEVs)

Among the most talked-about innovations in recent times, electric vehicles powered by batteries have made significant inroads in the market. Instead of an internal combustion engine burning fuel, BEVs run on electricity stored in large batteries. Charging these vehicles at home or dedicated stations, drivers are slowly getting accustomed to a world where "refueling" might mean plugging into an electric socket overnight.

Benefits:
- Zero tailpipe emissions, making them environmentally friendly in areas where electricity is generated from renewable sources.
- Quieter operations, leading to reduced noise pollution.
- Potential for lower operating costs, as electricity can be cheaper than gasoline or diesel.

The Middle Ground: Hybrid Vehicles

Hybrids are like the bridge between traditional gasoline vehicles and the future of electric cars. They contain both a small internal combustion engine and an electric motor powered by a battery. The vehicle smartly switches between the two, or sometimes uses both, optimizing performance and fuel efficiency.

Benefits:
- Improved fuel efficiency compared to traditional vehicles.
- Reduced emissions, especially in stop-and-go city driving where the electric motor can take over.
- A gentle introduction to electric vehicles without the worry of range anxiety.

Harnessing the Power of the Sun: Solar Vehicles

Solar vehicles utilize photovoltaic cells to convert sunlight into electricity, which either powers the car directly or charges its batteries. While not yet widespread for everyday use, solar vehicles have shown potential in specialized applications and racing events.

Benefits:
- Infinite fuel source as long as the sun shines.
- Zero emissions and a significant reduction in the carbon footprint.

From Waste to Wheels: Biofuels

Biofuels, like ethanol and biodiesel, are made from organic materials. Ethanol, typically produced from corn or sugarcane, can be blended with gasoline, while biodiesel, often derived from vegetable oils or animal fats, can be used in diesel engines.

Benefits:
- Renewable, as they're made from plants that can be grown every year.
- Potential for reduced greenhouse gas emissions.
- A possible boost to the agricultural sector, providing farmers with an additional source of income.

The Gas Alternative: Compressed Natural Gas (CNG) and Liquid Petroleum Gas (LPG)

Natural gas, when compressed, can serve as a cleaner alternative to gasoline. Similarly, LPG, a by-product of natural gas processing and petroleum refining, can be used.

Benefits:
- Lower emissions of harmful pollutants.
- Cheaper than gasoline in many regions.
- Abundant and domestically produced, reducing dependence on imported oil.

Fuel of the Future: Hydrogen and Fuel Cells

Hydrogen can be used in cars in two ways: by directly burning it in an engine, or more commonly, through a fuel cell. In fuel cells, hydrogen combines with oxygen from the air to produce electricity, which powers the vehicle.

Benefits:
- Only emission is water vapor, making it a zero-emission fuel.
- Potential for hydrogen to be produced from various domestic resources, including natural gas, nuclear power, biomass, and renewable power like solar and wind.

Navigating the New Frontier

The transportation landscape is rapidly evolving. While gasoline and diesel aren't going away anytime soon, the emergence of these alternative fuels represents a hopeful step towards a sustainable, environmentally conscious future.

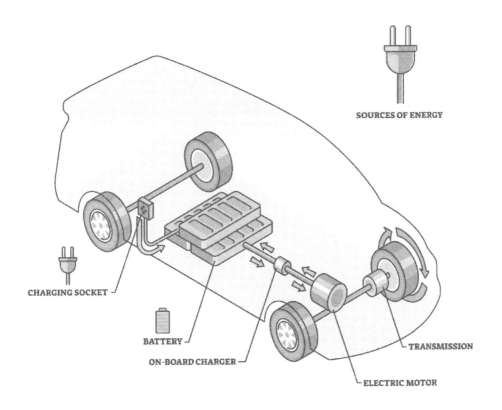

BEV
BATTERY ELECTRIC VEHICLE

SOURCES OF ENERGY

CHARGING SOCKET

BATTERY

ON-BOARD CHARGER

ELECTRIC MOTOR

TRANSMISSION

Chapter 10: The Rugged Diesel Engines

Fundamentals of Diesel Operation

When one hears the term "diesel," the images conjured often involve robust, powerful machinery, the rumbling of large trucks on highways, and the unmistakable hum of an engine built for endurance. Diesel engines, with their undeniable presence, have carved out a niche in the annals of automotive history, not merely as a source of power but as the very heartbeat of countless industries. To truly appreciate the marvel that is the diesel engine, we first need to venture deep into its fundamental operations.

Birth of the Diesel: Rudolf Diesel's Vision

In the late 19th century, German engineer Rudolf Diesel had a vision. Disturbed by the inefficiencies of the gasoline engines of his time, he envisioned an engine with a higher efficiency. After years of perseverance, in 1893, he gave birth to the diesel engine, an innovation that was destined to transform industries worldwide.

The Compression Ignition Principle: The Heart of Diesel Power

What sets diesel engines apart is the way they ignite fuel. Unlike gasoline engines, which rely on spark plugs to ignite a fuel-air mixture, diesel engines use the sheer force of compression. As air is drawn into the cylinder and compressed, its temperature soars, sometimes exceeding 540°C (1004°F). When diesel fuel is then injected into this super-hot compressed air, it spontaneously ignites. This principle is aptly named "compression ignition."

Why Diesel is Different: A Deep Dive into its Properties

If you've ever had a chance to feel diesel fuel, you might've noticed its oily texture. It's heavier and denser compared to gasoline. This density allows it to store more energy, contributing to the higher energy output and fuel efficiency commonly associated with diesel engines.

Moreover, diesel's boiling point is higher, meaning it's less volatile. This characteristic makes diesel engines less prone to knocking—a phenomenon where premature ignition occurs, which can be harmful to the engine.

Efficiency: The Diesel's Calling Card

One of diesel's most notable traits is its fuel efficiency. Diesel engines tend to have a higher thermal efficiency, which means they can convert more of the fuel's energy into mechanical power. This doesn't just translate to savings at the pump, but also reduced CO_2 emissions.

However, it's crucial to note that while diesels may emit less CO_2, they can produce more nitrogen oxides and particulates, leading to the development of technologies like particulate filters and selective catalytic reduction systems to combat these emissions.

Turbocharging and Diesel: A Match Made in Heaven

Modern diesel engines often come equipped with turbochargers. At its core, a turbocharger uses the engine's exhaust gas to spin a turbine, which then drives a compressor, forcing more air into the engine cylinders. This increased air allows the engine to burn fuel more efficiently, boosting power without increasing engine size.

The Cold Start Conundrum: Diesel's Achilles' Heel

While diesel engines have many strengths, they aren't without challenges. One such challenge is the infamous cold start issue. Because diesel engines rely on the heat generated from compressing air to ignite the fuel, starting the engine in colder temperatures, where the air doesn't heat as efficiently, can be problematic. Over the years, innovations like glow plugs, which preheat the air in the combustion chamber, have helped mitigate this issue.

Diesel's Role in the Modern World: Beyond Just Trucks

While many associate diesel primarily with heavy-duty trucks, its application is far more extensive. From generators that power events and backup essential facilities to marine applications powering boats and ships, diesel's reliability and efficiency have made it a favorite. Even passenger vehicles, sedans, and SUVs have adopted diesel, offering drivers the benefit of increased torque and fuel efficiency.

Treading into the Future: The Evolution Continues

Change is the only constant, and in the realm of engines, this axiom holds true. While diesel engines have been stalwarts for over a century, they too are evolving. With increasing emphasis on sustainability and environmental consciousness, diesel engines of today are cleaner, more efficient, and equipped with cutting-edge technologies.

Comparing Diesel to Gasoline Engines

Engines have always been the heart of any vehicle, pumping life and vigor into our cars, trucks, and machinery. Yet, not all engines are created equal. In the vast world of automotive powerhouses, two have always stood out, jostling for dominance and each boasting its unique advantages: Diesel and Gasoline. As we journey into this chapter, let's explore the intriguing contrasts and comparisons between these two stalwarts of the engine realm.

A History Rewind: Origins and Evolution
Before delving deep, it's essential to briefly touch upon how these two engines came into being. Gasoline engines preceded their diesel counterparts, with early prototypes appearing in the mid-19th century. Diesel engines made their debut towards the end of the same century, envisioned by Rudolf Diesel as a more efficient alternative.

The Combustion Chronicles: How They Work
At their core, both engines convert fuel into energy through combustion. However, the methods differ.
Gasoline engines employ an external source, typically a spark plug, to ignite a mixture of fuel and air. This method, aptly termed "spark ignition," relies on precise timing to ensure smooth operation.
Diesel engines, as we discussed in the previous section, utilize the "compression ignition" method. Relying on the heat generated by compressed air, diesel engines spontaneously ignite the injected fuel, eliminating the need for an external ignition source.

Efficiency & Power: Where Diesel Takes the Lead
Diesel engines shine when it comes to torque and fuel efficiency. Their higher compression ratios and the energy-rich nature of diesel fuel allow them to extract more power from each fuel drop. This translates to better fuel economy and a more substantial low-end torque, making them especially suitable for hauling heavy loads.

Emissions & Environment: A Balance of Scales
Environmental considerations have become paramount in today's world. Gasoline engines generally produce less nitrogen oxide and particulates, making them appear cleaner. However, they emit more carbon dioxide due to lower fuel efficiency.

Diesel engines, conversely, are champions in carbon dioxide emissions, emitting less due to their efficiency. But they have historically struggled with nitrogen oxides and particulates, prompting the development of advanced emission control technologies.

Performance & Responsiveness: Gasoline's Playground

For those who crave immediate throttle response and high RPM adventures, gasoline engines have been the go-to. Their ability to rev high and provide instant power makes them a favorite among performance enthusiasts.

While modern diesel engines have made significant strides in responsiveness and overall performance, gasoline engines still often have the edge in high-speed applications and rapid acceleration.

Maintenance & Longevity: Diesel's Long Road Ahead

When it comes to endurance, diesel engines are often touted as the more robust option. Their robust construction to handle high compression ratios means they're built to last. Additionally, diesel's inherent lubrication properties can contribute to longer engine life.

However, this durability often comes with a caveat: maintenance. Diesel engines can be more expensive to maintain, primarily due to their complex emission control systems and the need to manage diesel particulates.

Cost Implications: An Ongoing Debate

Historically, diesel fuel was cheaper than gasoline, making diesel engines an economical choice for many, especially those clocking in higher mileages. However, fluctuations in global oil markets and the increasing cost of refining diesel have sometimes reversed this trend.

Moreover, while diesel vehicles often come with higher upfront costs due to their robust construction, the potential savings in fuel and longevity might offset this for some users.

The Four Strokes of Diesel Efficiency

1. Intake: Breathing Life into the Engine

Every journey begins with a single step, and for the diesel engine, it starts with a breath. The intake stroke initiates the process, as the engine takes in a lungful of fresh air. The piston, starting at the top, descends into the cylinder, creating a vacuum that draws in air through the open intake valve. This simple yet crucial action ensures that there's enough oxygen present for the upcoming combustion.

2. Compression: The Build-Up of Anticipation

If the intake stroke is the gentle inhale, the compression stroke is the held breath before the climax. As the intake valve closes, the piston begins its upward journey, compressing the captured air within the confines of the cylinder.

It's this phase that gives the diesel engine its distinctive trait: the ability to achieve very high compression ratios. As the air gets squeezed, its temperature rises dramatically. By the end of this stroke, conditions within the cylinder are ripe for ignition, with air temperatures soaring, eagerly awaiting the fuel's introduction.

3. Power: The Grand Performance

With the stage set and the players ready, the power stroke heralds the engine's main event. Right at the culmination of the compression stroke, with the piston near the top of the cylinder, a precise squirt of diesel fuel is injected into this superheated air. Almost immediately, the fuel spontaneously ignites, given the high temperatures.

The resultant explosion from the combustion exerts a force on the piston, driving it downward with considerable power. This downstroke, propelled by the force of the combustion, converts the stored potential energy from the fuel into kinetic energy, which in turn drives the engine's crankshaft and, eventually, propels the vehicle.

4. Exhaust: The Elegant Conclusion

With the grand performance complete, the engine must now prepare for the next cycle. The exhaust stroke serves as the graceful finale of our mechanical ballet. As the piston begins its upward trajectory after the power stroke, the exhaust valve opens.

This action allows the spent combustion gases, the remnants of the earlier explosion, to be expelled from the cylinder. It's akin to a sigh after an intense performance, ridding the system of waste and resetting the stage for the next act.

Harmony and Efficiency: The Diesel's Signature

These four strokes, while seemingly straightforward, represent the culmination of more than a century of engineering refinement. Their precise coordination ensures the diesel engine's trademark efficiency and torque. The high compression ratios lead to a more complete combustion, harnessing more of the fuel's potential energy and converting it into motion. Moreover, this cycle's continuous repetition, happening countless times every minute, emphasizes the durability and resilience of diesel engines. Every phase, from intake to exhaust, must occur flawlessly to ensure optimal performance, highlighting the engine's fine-tuned nature.

Chapter 11: The Future is Hybrid

Breaking Down Hybrid Technology

At its core, the essence of a hybrid vehicle lies in its dual power sources: the gasoline engine and the electric motor. Like a symphony with two leading instruments, they harmonize, sometimes playing together and sometimes allowing the other to take the lead, ensuring the music – in this case, the journey – continues uninterrupted.

The Gasoline Engine: Just as in a traditional car, the gasoline engine in a hybrid is there for power. It provides that reassuring purr and responsive acceleration when you press the accelerator. But unlike in traditional vehicles, this engine often works in tandem with, or sometimes takes a back seat to, its electric counterpart.

The Electric Motor: A marvel of modern engineering, the electric motor in a hybrid can both power the car independently and act as an assistant to the gasoline engine. The magic of the electric motor is its ability to deliver power instantly, offering smooth and quiet acceleration.

Energy on Demand: Intelligent Transitioning

One might wonder, how does the vehicle decide when to utilize its electric motor or its gasoline engine? The hybrid's computerized brain is continually assessing the best source of power. For instance, during times of heavy acceleration or when climbing a steep hill, both the engine and motor might be called upon. In contrast, cruising at a steady speed on a flat road might be left entirely to the electric motor.

Recapturing Lost Energy: Regenerative Braking

A gem in the hybrid's crown is its ability to recapture energy typically lost during braking. Think about the energy wasted in heat and sound when we apply brakes. Hybrid systems use a process called "regenerative braking." Instead of just using traditional brake pads to slow the vehicle, the electric motor can run in reverse, turning the wheels' kinetic energy back into electrical power and storing it in the battery for later use. It's like having a little power plant on wheels, always looking for ways to conserve and reuse energy.

Battery – The Silent Guardian

No discussion of hybrids would be complete without mentioning the battery, the silent guardian in the ensemble. The battery stores energy for the electric motor. But don't confuse this with the tiny battery in traditional cars that start the engine and power the radio. This is a much larger, high-capacity battery designed to store and deliver significant amounts of energy. And fear not, for the vehicle is always monitoring the battery's health, ensuring it's charged and ready for action without you having to plug it in.

Optimized Fuel Efficiency: The Payoff

All this technology has one main goal: to save fuel. The delicate dance between gasoline engine and electric motor ensures that hybrids often consume much less fuel than their non-hybrid counterparts. When you're stuck in traffic, instead of guzzling gas while idling, the gasoline engine can shut off entirely, letting the electric motor and battery handle the minimal power needs. On the highway, when more power is required, the gasoline engine can take over, ensuring you always have the acceleration and speed you need.

Reduced Emissions: A Breath of Fresh Air

Beyond just saving at the pump, hybrids are an environmentally conscious choice. With a reduced reliance on gasoline and increased use of clean electric power, they emit fewer pollutants and greenhouse gases. Every hybrid on the road is a step towards cleaner air and a healthier planet.

A Glimpse Into Evolution: Why Hybrids Matter

Hybrid technology represents more than just a new type of car; it signifies a critical step in automotive evolution. As we face dwindling fossil fuel reserves and increased environmental concerns, the move toward more sustainable modes of transport becomes imperative. Hybrids, in seamlessly integrating the old with the new, provide a practical and efficient solution, ensuring we don't have to compromise on performance as we stride into a greener future.

Benefits and Maintenance Tips

Diving into the world of hybrids is akin to stepping into a realm where tradition meets innovation. It's the best of both worlds, but with the union comes an array of benefits that cater to both our practical needs and our environmental responsibilities.

Financial Savings: A Wallet's Best Friend

Fuel Efficiency: It's no secret that one of the most celebrated advantages of driving a hybrid is the notable increase in fuel efficiency. With the intelligent system deciding when to switch between gasoline and electric power, hybrids ensure optimal use of energy. This means fewer trips to the gas station and more money saved.

Tax Incentives and Rebates: Governments around the world are eager to promote eco-friendly driving. Many countries and states offer tax incentives, rebates, or discounts for hybrid car owners, further enhancing the financial attractiveness of making the switch.

Planet Protectors: An Eco-Friendly Choice

Reduced Greenhouse Gas Emissions: Less reliance on gasoline means fewer emissions. Driving a hybrid sends a clear message: you care about reducing your carbon footprint and playing an active role in combating global warming.

Less Noise Pollution: The whisper-quiet operation of the electric motor, especially at lower speeds, means a significant reduction in noise pollution. Imagine a future with bustling streets that are serene, thanks to the quiet hum of hybrids.

Performance Paired with Responsibility

Seamless Acceleration: Contrary to some myths, hybrids don't compromise on performance. The instant torque provided by electric motors can give hybrids a zippy feel, especially during city drives.

Smooth Transitions: Modern hybrids have refined the transition between their gasoline and electric power sources, ensuring drivers experience smooth and seamless shifts, enhancing overall driving pleasure.

Adapting to Hybrid Maintenance: Keeping the Future Bright

Hybrids, with their unique makeup, demand a slightly different maintenance approach compared to traditional vehicles. Here's a handy guide to ensure your hybrid remains in top-notch condition.

Monitoring the Battery: The Powerhouse

Unlike the standard battery in conventional vehicles, hybrid batteries are designed for longevity. However, it's crucial to keep an eye on its health. Most hybrids come with battery health indicators. Regularly checking these indicators can alert you to any potential issues.

Brake System: Longer Life but Don't Neglect

Thanks to regenerative braking, the physical brake system in hybrids often lasts longer than in non-hybrids. Nevertheless, it's wise to have them inspected during routine check-ups. Remember, while the regenerative system does a lot, it's the physical brakes that provide the final stopping power.

Oil Changes: Stick to the Schedule

Hybrids might use their gasoline engines less frequently, but regular oil changes are still a must. The good news? Many hybrids often have longer intervals between oil changes due to reduced wear and tear. Always refer to the owner's manual for the manufacturer's recommendation.

Cooling System: An Overlooked Hero

The cooling system in a hybrid doesn't just cater to the engine. It also ensures the battery stays at an optimal temperature. Regularly checking the coolant levels and ensuring the system is functioning effectively can extend the battery's life.

Regular Software Check-ups

Modern hybrids heavily rely on computer systems to manage their dual power sources. It's beneficial to have software diagnostics run during regular maintenance visits to ensure everything is communicating and functioning as it should.

Hybrid Cars: The Road Ahead

It's a fascinating time to be alive in the world of automotive technology. The streets that once echoed with the roars of gasoline engines are now punctuated with the soft hums of hybrids. From a niche market segment to becoming a substantial portion of cars on the road today, hybrids have certainly come a long way. But where is this journey taking us? What does the horizon hold for these marvels of automotive engineering?

The Proliferation of Models: A Spectrum of Choices

Initially, only a few car models were available for those looking to go hybrid. But the scenario today is wildly different. Nearly every major automaker has incorporated hybrids into their lineup, and some have even announced ambitious plans to electrify their entire range in the coming decades.

This proliferation isn't just in numbers but also in variety. From compact cars to SUVs and luxury models, there's a hybrid for every taste and need. As technology continues to evolve, the line between traditional and hybrid vehicles will blur, offering consumers the aesthetic and performance they desire, along with the eco-friendly benefits of hybrid technology.

Integration of Advanced Tech: Smart Hybrids

Cars today aren't just about transportation; they're about connectivity, automation, and personalization. Future hybrid models will seamlessly integrate with our digital lives. Think of vehicles that sync with your calendar, suggesting the best routes for your day's appointments, or cars that adapt their performance profiles based on the music you're listening to.

Moreover, as autonomous driving technologies advance, hybrids will be at the forefront. Their electric components mesh well with the sensors and processors required for self-driving, making them prime candidates for these innovations.

Environmental Impact: A Green Revival

The environmental benefits of hybrids are clear, but the future holds even more promise. Research is continuously seeking ways to make batteries more efficient, longer-lasting, and environmentally friendly. There's ongoing work on 'green' batteries that are made from more sustainable materials and are easier to recycle.

Moreover, as the energy grid itself becomes cleaner, with an increased reliance on renewable sources like wind and solar, the environmental advantage of hybrids will magnify. Imagine a world where hybrids run primarily on electricity derived from renewable sources, making them almost entirely carbon-neutral.

Infrastructure and Support: A Growing Ecosystem
The future of hybrid cars is closely tied to the infrastructure that supports them. As hybrids become mainstream, we can anticipate a surge in hybrid-specific services and facilities. This could range from more hybrid-friendly mechanics and repair shops to urban planning that incorporates hybrid car needs, like specialized lanes or charging stations.
Moreover, there's an exciting potential for vehicle-to-grid (V2G) systems. Here, hybrids could feed excess energy back into the grid during times of low usage, turning them into mobile power storage units that contribute to the community's energy needs.

It's tempting to view the future of hybrid cars through a lens of pure optimism, and indeed, there's much to be hopeful for. However, challenges remain, from creating truly sustainable battery solutions to managing the socioeconomic implications of a shift away from traditional fuels.

Chapter 12: Guiding and Supporting: Steering and Suspension

Comprehensive Overview

It's the steering system that lets you dictate your car's path. Every time you turn the wheel, a series of components spring into action, ensuring your car responds to your command.

The steering wheel connects to a shaft, which then leads to a gear assembly. This gear assembly amplifies your steering effort, making it easier to turn the wheels. The final connection to the wheels is through tie rods, ensuring a synchronized movement. It's a continuous chain of communication, from your hands on the steering wheel to the tires on the road.

Now, steering isn't just about left or right. It's about precision and feedback. You want to feel connected to the road, understanding its nuances, and adjusting accordingly. This balance is achieved through the type of steering system in use:

- **Hydraulic Power Steering (HPS):** Traditionally, many cars used HPS, which employs hydraulic fluid to aid in steering. As you turn the wheel, a pump pressurizes the fluid, which then helps move the steering gear, lightening your effort.

- **Electronic Power Steering (EPS):** Modern vehicles are leaning towards EPS. Instead of relying on hydraulic fluid, it uses electric motors to assist your steering efforts. EPS can adapt to different driving conditions and generally offers more feedback to the driver.

The Unsung Hero: The Suspension System

While the steering system is about command and control, the suspension system is all about comfort and stability. It's what stands between you and every bump, pothole, or rough patch on the road.

Your car's suspension is an intricate network of springs, shock absorbers, and linkages that connect the vehicle to its wheels. Its primary function? To offer support while absorbing any disturbances the road might introduce.

When you drive over a bump, the springs compress, absorbing much of the initial impact. As they expand back, shock absorbers (or dampers) come into play, controlling the bounce and ensuring your tires remain in contact with the road.

But it's not just about absorbing shocks. The suspension system also maintains the right wheel alignment, ensures optimal tire contact, and controls the vehicle's direction in motion. In essence, while you lead with the steering wheel, the suspension system makes sure your car follows that lead gracefully.

Harmony in Motion

Your car's movement is a symphony of forces. As you cruise down the highway or navigate tight city corners, both steering and suspension systems are hard at work, ensuring you remain in control. They are, in many ways, the unsung heroes of your driving experience.

Imagine driving without a responsive steering system. Each turn would be a gamble, and sharp bends could become treacherous. Now, think of a drive without an effective suspension system. Every minor road imperfection would jolt you, making drives uncomfortable, if not downright painful.

But together, these systems work in tandem, offering a balance of command and comfort. They ensure that you're not just traveling from point A to B, but you're doing so with confidence and ease.

DIY Tips for the Steering System

Many car enthusiasts love the idea of being one with their vehicle, understanding its nuances, and being hands-on. But when it comes to the steering system, many shy away, thinking it too complex or delicate. Let's debunk that myth today. While certain tasks are better left to professionals, there are aspects of the steering system you can monitor and even address on your own.

Setting the Scene: Safety First

Before diving deep into the realm of DIY, it's imperative to ensure safety. Always ensure that:

1. Your car is on a flat and stable surface.
2. You're equipped with the right tools for the job.
3. The vehicle's ignition is turned off, and the keys are safely out of reach.

4. You have protective gloves and safety glasses on.

Getting a Feel: Checking for Play
One of the first signs that something might be amiss with your steering system is a noticeable "play" or "slack" in the steering wheel. You can check this at home:

Position yourself in the driver's seat with your hands on the steering wheel. Gently move the wheel from side to side, without turning on the engine. If there's significant movement without resistance, it might be an indicator of wear in the steering components.

Hear and Observe: Noise and Uneven Tire Wear
Another simple yet effective DIY tip is to observe. Listen for any unusual noises when you turn the steering wheel. A creaking, knocking, or groaning sound might indicate problems with the steering rack or tie rods. Similarly, uneven tire wear can be a sign of misalignment or issues with the steering components. A quick visual inspection of your tires every once in a while can alert you to potential issues.

Power Steering Fluid: The Lifeblood
For vehicles equipped with Hydraulic Power Steering (HPS), the fluid is crucial. It's the medium that facilitates the easy turn of the steering wheel. Checking and topping up this fluid can be a straightforward DIY task:

Locate the power steering reservoir under your hood (usually labeled). Check the fluid level against the markers on the reservoir. If it's below the 'MIN' mark, you'll need to top it up with the recommended fluid type. Remember, overfilling can be just as harmful as under-filling, so always aim for the 'MAX' mark.

Cleanliness is Key: Keeping it Clean
Over time, debris, dust, and dirt can accumulate in the components of the steering system. While it might seem minor, this build-up can lead to wear and tear over time. A simple DIY tip is to occasionally give the steering components a gentle wipe-down. Using a damp cloth, gently clean around the steering rack, pinion, and tie rods. This not only prolongs their life but also allows you to spot any potential leaks or damages.

Tightening the Bonds: Checking Bolts and Connections
It might surprise you how often minor steering issues are a result of loose bolts or connections. A routine check, using a simple wrench, can ensure that everything is tight and in place. While you don't want to over-tighten, ensuring that there's no excessive "give" in these components can save you from bigger issues down the road.

When to Put the Wrench Down: Recognizing Limits
While DIY can be both fun and rewarding, it's equally essential to recognize its limits. Some tasks, like realigning wheels, replacing worn-out tie rods, or handling intricate electronic components in modern Electronic Power Steering (EPS) systems, require professional hands. Recognizing when to seek professional help can save both your wallet and potential mishaps with your vehicle.

When to Turn to Professionals

While certain signs like a vibrating steering wheel or noticeable play might guide you to investigate further, some issues remain more clandestine. For instance, if your vehicle seems to drift to one side even when you think you're driving straight or if the steering feels unusually stiff, these could be indicative of deeper underlying issues—ones that require a seasoned mechanic's diagnostic skills.

The Tools and Tech Advantage
Professionals don't just bring experience to the table; they also have an arsenal of specialized tools and technology. Modern-day cars, with their plethora of sensors and electronic systems, can throw up diagnostic codes that only professional-grade scanners can read. So, while you might notice a symptom, the root cause could be hidden deep within, decipherable only with the right tools.

Aligning Priorities: Wheel Alignment
Ever noticed uneven tire wear or that your vehicle tends to pull towards one side? It could be a wheel alignment issue. While the symptoms are easy to spot, the alignment process itself is intricate, requiring specialized machinery and expertise. An alignment rack, coupled with a professional's keen eye, ensures your wheels are perfectly aligned, offering optimal handling and extended tire life.

Steering Overhauls and Major Repairs

Sometimes, the problem goes beyond a simple adjustment or part replacement. For instance, if the steering rack, a central component, is damaged or worn out, it's a task that goes beyond the DIY realm. Replacing or repairing such a significant part requires precision, as even slight misalignments can affect the vehicle's overall handling and safety.

Safety First: The Non-Negotiables

Certain components of the steering system directly impact the safety of the vehicle. The tie rods, for example, play a pivotal role in connecting the steering system to the wheels. If they were to malfunction or break while driving, the results could be catastrophic. While routine checks and maintenance are encouraged, any doubts about critical components should be immediately addressed by professionals.

Warranty Wonders and Pitfalls

Modern vehicles often come with warranties that cover various components, including the steering system. While it's tempting to dive in and fix an issue, doing so without proper knowledge might void the warranty. Always check your vehicle's warranty terms. Sometimes, taking it to a professional not only ensures the job is done right but also keeps your warranty intact.

Chapter 13: Tires – The Legs of Your Car

Understanding Alignment and Its Importance

In essence, wheel alignment refers to the adjustments of your vehicle's wheels to ensure they are parallel to each other and perpendicular to the ground. It might sound straightforward, but these angles influence the way your vehicle handles, the lifespan of your tires, and even the efficiency of your fuel consumption.

Aligning with Purpose: The Significance
Let's explore the profound impact of wheel alignment on different aspects of your vehicle:

Ensuring A Smooth Ride:
Proper wheel alignment ensures that your car drives straight without pulling to one side. This translates to a more comfortable driving experience. It's the difference between gliding down the road and wrestling with your steering wheel.

Optimizing Tire Lifespan:
Misaligned wheels can cause your tires to wear unevenly and prematurely. It's not just about saving money on frequent tire replacements; it's also about ensuring safety. Uneven tire wear can reduce grip, making your vehicle less safe on the road, especially in wet conditions.

Fuel Efficiency:
Believe it or not, wheel alignment can influence your car's fuel efficiency. When wheels are not aligned, they can create uneven and additional resistance, making your engine work harder and burn more fuel.

The Intricacies of Alignment: Camber, Caster, and Toe
Wheel alignment might seem simple at first glance, but it is a delicate balance of adjustments. Let's delve into the nuances:

Camber:
Think about viewing your car from the front. Camber pertains to the tilt of

the top of your tires. If they lean towards the car, it's negative camber. If they lean away, it's positive. Incorrect camber can lead to wear on one side of the tire.

Caster:
Now imagine viewing your car from the side. Caster involves the angle of the steering pivot. A forward tilt is negative, while a backward tilt is positive. This angle impacts steering stability and cornering.

Toe:
Again, from a bird's eye view, if the fronts of the tires are closer together than the backs, they have toe-in. If the backs are closer, they have toe-out. The correct toe setting ensures even tire wear and a straight trajectory.

A Tale of Misalignment: Telltale Signs
Your car communicates with you, sometimes subtly, sometimes more overtly. When it comes to misalignment, here are a few stories it might tell:

A Drifting Tale:
If your vehicle drifts to one side despite your best efforts to steer it straight, it's beckoning for a wheel alignment check.

The Uneven Chronicles:
Your tires share their wear patterns, a visible tale of their journey. If one side of a tire wears faster than the other, it's signaling misalignment.

A Song of Vibrations:
If your steering wheel vibrates, especially at certain speeds, it might be singing the song of misaligned wheels.

Signs and Solutions for Misalignment

Every seasoned car owner knows that vehicles, in their unique way, communicate. While they don't use words, they give us signals, nudges, and sometimes desperate cries for attention. Misalignment, often an elusive culprit, manifests its presence through various signs. Recognizing these early can save time, money, and ensure safer journeys.

Decoding the Signs of Misalignment

Steering Sideways:
If your steering wheel isn't centered when you're driving straight, it's more than just a minor annoyance; it's your car's subtle way of indicating a misalignment. A centered steering wheel is not just about aesthetics; it's an assurance that your wheels and steering system are in harmony.

Turn and Burn:
Notice your tires wearing out faster than usual? Or perhaps only on one edge? This rapid or uneven wear is a telltale sign of misalignment. It's not just your wallet that feels the pinch with frequent tire replacements; it's also a crucial safety concern. Properly aligned tires wear at a uniform rate, ensuring consistent traction across all wheels.

The Steering Struggle:
A vehicle in its prime should glide on the road with minimal effort. If your car resists your steering or seems to have a mind of its own, wandering off to the sides, it's an urgent nudge to check the alignment.

The Vibrating Veil:
Experiencing a persistent vibration in the steering wheel can be disconcerting. While many culprits can cause this, from imbalanced tires to issues with the brake system, misalignment is a prominent player in the vibrating game.

Restoring Balance: Solutions for Misalignment
Understanding the problem is half the battle; the other half lies in crafting effective solutions. Let's unravel the path to rectifying misalignment:

Routine Inspections:
The adage, "Prevention is better than cure," holds weight here. Regularly scheduled alignment checks, especially after any significant jolts from potholes or curbs, can catch issues before they escalate.

Professional Calibration:
Wheel alignment is a delicate dance of measurements and adjustments. While the DIY spirit is commendable, alignment requires specialized equipment and expertise. It's more than just adjusting wheels; it's about ensuring the entire steering and suspension systems are in harmony.

Replace Worn Components:
Often, misalignment is a symptom of an underlying issue. Worn out or damaged parts in the suspension or steering system can throw your alignment off balance. Regularly inspect and replace parts like tie rods, ball joints, and bushings to ensure a smoothly operating system.

Tyre Maintenance:
While not a direct solution to alignment, maintaining your tires - ensuring they're properly inflated, routinely rotated, and replaced when worn - can enhance the effectiveness of an alignment job and prolong its benefits.

Beyond the Technical: The Aesthetics of Aligned Driving
There's a tangible pleasure in driving a well-aligned car. The ride is smoother, the steering more responsive, and the overall experience more harmonious. Misalignment, in contrast, brings discord to this symphony.
The alignment of your vehicle isn't just about technicalities and wear patterns; it's about the sheer joy of driving. It's about the confidence in knowing your vehicle will respond to your commands, the assurance of safety in its grip on the road, and the satisfaction of a journey free from jarring vibrations or constant steering corrections.

The Lifelong Benefits of Proper Tire Care

The wheels of your vehicle, quite literally, carry the weight of your journeys. They're the point of contact between the aspirations of the driver and the raw, unyielding roads of the world. When well-maintained, they form a harmonious bond with the asphalt, offering a seamless driving experience. But if neglected, they can become a vehicle's Achilles' heel. Let's explore the myriad benefits that come with consistent and thoughtful tire care.

Longevity: More Than Just Mileage

Economically Efficient:
Taking care of your tires is akin to an investment. The more attention you give them, the fewer replacements you'll need over the vehicle's lifetime. Properly cared-for tires wear down more slowly, ensuring that you extract every mile from them, providing a return on your investment.

Consistent Performance:
A well-maintained tire delivers optimal performance. Whether it's braking on wet roads, navigating sharp turns, or simply cruising on a sunny day, the tire's grip, responsiveness, and overall performance remain consistent, ensuring that the vehicle behaves predictably in various conditions.

Safety: A Paramount Concern

Optimal Traction:
Tires in good condition ensure maximum traction, a critical factor in inclement weather. When roads are slick with rain or treacherous with snow, well-maintained tires can be the difference between a close call and an unfortunate incident.

Preventing Blowouts:
Worn-out or damaged tires are more susceptible to blowouts. Regular inspections can identify vulnerabilities, such as bulges or deep cuts, allowing timely replacements and reducing the risk of sudden tire failures.

Fuel Efficiency: Rolling Towards Savings
Well-maintained tires roll more efficiently on the road, minimizing resistance. This efficiency translates directly into better fuel economy.

By keeping your tires in top shape, you're not only ensuring a smooth drive but also visiting the gas station less frequently, leading to considerable savings over time.

The Quiet Comfort of a Smooth Ride
A car with well-maintained tires simply feels better to drive. It offers a smoother ride, free from the jarring bumps and jolts that can come from uneven tire wear. Moreover, properly inflated and balanced tires produce less road noise, allowing for a quieter and more comfortable driving experience.

The Environmental Angle
Proper tire care isn't just beneficial to the car owner; it's a boon for the environment too. Efficient tires mean better fuel economy, leading to fewer emissions. Additionally, extending the life of your tires reduces the frequency of tire disposal, easing the burden on landfills.

Chapter 14: Emergency Roadside Situations

Preparedness: Your Best Ally

Imagine this: It's a sunny afternoon, and you're cruising along the highway, listening to your favorite playlist, feeling the warm breeze on your face. The open road lies ahead, and everything seems perfect. But suddenly, an unfamiliar light flickers on the dashboard, or perhaps there's an unexpected sputter from the engine. In moments like these, the security of the familiar is replaced with the anxiety of the unexpected. However, with preparation, that anxiety can be significantly reduced, if not completely alleviated.

Being Ready: More Than Just a Mantra

Staying Ahead with Information:
Knowledge is a powerful tool. Understanding your vehicle's basic operations, its warning signals, and knowing some fundamental troubleshooting can transform unexpected breakdowns from full-blown crises into manageable situations. Always keep a vehicle manual in your glove compartment. It might seem outdated in this age of digital everything, but when signals go awry, that manual can become your lifeline.

Emergency Kits - A Necessary Companion:
Every vehicle should be equipped with an emergency kit. It should contain essentials like jumper cables, a flashlight, basic tools, water bottles, non-perishable snacks, a first-aid kit, and reflective triangles or flares. For those in colder climates, add items like a blanket, ice scraper, and even cat litter (yes, it can help provide traction on slick surfaces). But having an emergency kit isn't enough; you must ensure that everything in it is in good condition and ready for use.

Training: Not Just for Professionals

Emergencies can strike anyone, and while professionals handle them daily, every driver should possess a basic understanding of emergency procedures. Consider taking a basic car maintenance or roadside emergency class. Knowledge, combined with hands-on experience, can boost your confidence, ensuring you remain calm and collected during an emergency.

Mapping It Out

Modern technology has given us GPS, but relying solely on digital navigation can sometimes lead to complications, especially in remote areas with poor signal reception. Keep a physical map in your car. It might sound old-fashioned, but being able to chart a course without digital assistance can sometimes be crucial.

Anticipating the Worst-Case Scenarios

While we hope they never happen, thinking about potential emergencies can better prepare us for them. For instance:

Waterlogged Roads:
Driving during a downpour can be challenging, but what if you encounter a flooded road? Knowing beforehand that it's unsafe to drive through flooded areas, no matter how shallow they seem, can prevent the calamity of getting stuck or worse.

Snowy Surprises:
Snowstorms can be both beautiful and treacherous. Understanding the importance of reducing speed, increasing following distance, and the dangers of black ice can make all the difference.

Deserted and Alone:
If you're traveling through a remote area and your vehicle breaks down, knowing to stay with your car (it's easier to spot than a person) can keep you safe until help arrives.

The Power of Communication

In today's interconnected world, it's easier than ever to keep loved ones informed. Before embarking on long journeys, inform someone about your route and expected arrival time. If something goes wrong, they'll have an idea of where to start looking. Furthermore, always ensure your phone is charged when traveling, and consider investing in a car charger or portable power bank.

A Lifeline in Technology

Many modern vehicles come with built-in emergency response systems. Familiarize yourself with these services if your vehicle offers them. There are also numerous apps available that can send out emergency alerts, share your location, or even guide you through first aid procedures. Embrace this technology, but remember not to rely solely on it.

The Harmony of Preparedness and Peace of Mind

As we traverse the myriad paths that crisscross our vast world, the unexpected is an inevitable companion. However, with the right preparation, it doesn't have to be an unwelcome one. Preparedness doesn't just provide tools and procedures; it gives peace of mind, a calm assurance that whatever the road throws at you, you're ready for it.

Emergencies don't announce their arrival. But in the dance between chaos and control, preparedness ensures that we lead, making the journey not just about the destination but the confidence and serenity with which we reach it.

Managing Different Emergency Scenarios

To manage any crisis effectively, one must first understand its nature. On the road, emergencies can range from minor inconveniences to life-threatening situations. While every scenario is unique, having a mental toolkit of strategies can often be the difference between escalating a problem and finding a solution.

When the Engine Quits Mid-Drive

It's a driver's nightmare: cruising at highway speeds when suddenly, the engine dies. Panic can quickly set in, but it's essential to stay calm.

1. **Staying in Control:** Grip the steering wheel firmly. Without engine power, the power steering will be unresponsive, but you can still steer the vehicle—though it will require more effort.

2. **Safe Space:** Signal and maneuver your car to the shoulder or a safe spot off the road. Avoid braking hard or suddenly, as it can cause a loss of control.

3. **Alert Others:** Once safely off the road, turn on your hazard lights to indicate to other drivers that there's a problem.

A Tire Blowout on the Freeway

The loud bang, the sudden jerk of the car—it's unmistakable. A tire blowout at high speeds can be dangerous but manageable.

1. **Maintain Course:** Your first instinct might be to brake or swerve, but it's vital to keep the car going straight. Gently ease off the accelerator and maintain a grip on the steering wheel.

2. **Signal and Move:** Once you've decreased your speed considerably, signal and move carefully to the roadside or any safe space.

3. **Replace or Call:** If you're comfortable doing so and have a spare tire, replace the blown-out tire. If not, it's time to call for roadside assistance.

When Visibility Drops

Driving through fog, heavy rain, or snow can drastically reduce visibility. In such conditions, it's crucial to:

1. **Reduce Speed:** It might seem obvious, but slowing down gives you more reaction time and reduces the chance of an accident.

2. **Lights On, but Not High Beams:** In fog or heavy rain, high beams can reflect off the droplets and impair visibility further. Instead, use your regular headlights.

3. **Increase Following Distance:** This gives you more time to react to sudden stops or obstacles on the road.

Unanticipated Animal Crossings

Deer, raccoons, and other wildlife can suddenly dash onto roads, especially in rural or wooded areas. If an animal jumps in front of your vehicle:

1. **Do Not Swerve Violently:** It can cause you to lose control or veer into oncoming traffic.

2. **Brake Firmly and Steadily:** If a collision seems inevitable, it's safer to hit the animal than to swerve into oncoming traffic or off the road.

3. **Be Especially Vigilant at Dawn and Dusk:** Many animals are most active during these times.

Getting Stuck in Mud or Snow

It can happen during an adventurous detour or an unexpected storm.

1. **Avoid Spinning Your Wheels:** This can dig you in deeper. Instead, try to move the car slowly back and forth using the highest gear possible.

2. **Traction Aids:** Use mats, gravel, sand, or even cat litter beneath the tires to gain traction.

3. **Deflate the Tires:** Letting out some air can increase the tire's surface area, improving traction. Remember to inflate them again once you're free.

Every road trip, long or short, is an adventure filled with its set of challenges. While we cannot predict every hurdle we might face, we can arm ourselves with knowledge and presence of mind.

The Role of Authorities in Accidents

Emergencies on the road, especially accidents, often bring with them a flurry of emotions: panic, shock, confusion, and sometimes even anger. While it's natural for these feelings to flood in, it's crucial to remind ourselves of the immediate action to take: ensure safety.

Before diving into the role of authorities, remember to check if you or any of your passengers are injured. If anyone is hurt, no matter how minor it might seem, prioritizing medical attention is paramount. Once everyone's immediate safety is confirmed, the next step is to involve the authorities.

The Call to the Police

Any significant road accident should involve the police. Even if the damages seem minor or if both parties agree on what transpired, having an official record can be invaluable.

1. **Documentation:** Police will file an accident report, which provides an official account of the incident. This report becomes a crucial piece of documentation when dealing with insurance claims or any potential legal issues.

2. **Neutral Mediation:** Emotions can run high after an accident. The presence of a police officer can help mediate the situation, ensuring that interactions between the involved parties remain civil.

Emergency Medical Services (EMS)

In cases of injury, EMS personnel provide the immediate medical care needed before reaching a hospital. Their role is to stabilize, treat, and transport those who are injured. The golden hour, the first hour after an accident, is critical for many injuries. EMS professionals are trained to make the most of this time, increasing the chances of a positive outcome.

Firefighters: Not Just for Fires

While primarily associated with combating fires, firefighters also play a significant role at the scene of an accident, especially if there's a risk of a fire from leaking fuel or if individuals are trapped inside vehicles. Their tools and training allow them to extract people from wrecked cars safely.

Roadside Assistance and Tow Services

Once the immediate safety and medical concerns are addressed, the focus shifts to the vehicles. If they're not in drivable condition, you'll need the services of a tow truck. Some authorities will have specific tow services they work with, especially if the vehicle poses a hazard in its current location.

Legal Implications and Authorities

Depending on the severity of the accident and the region, legal authorities might also play a role. It's always a good idea to be familiar with local traffic laws, especially when traveling in unfamiliar areas.

1. **Legal Representation:** If you believe the accident wasn't your fault or if there are significant injuries or damages involved, it might be wise to consult with a legal professional. They can guide you through the complexities of traffic laws and potential legal proceedings.

2. **Insurance Claims:** Your insurance company becomes a key player post-accident. The police report, photographs of the scene, and accounts from any witnesses can be invaluable when filing a claim. It's essential to report the accident to your insurance provider as soon as possible.

Maintaining Perspective and Gratitude

In the aftermath of an accident, it's easy to get lost in the stress, blame, and chaos. Yet, it's crucial to take a moment and acknowledge the swift response and aid provided by various authorities. From the police officer who documents the scene to the EMS professional ensuring your well-being, each plays a role in turning a traumatic event into a structured path towards recovery.

Chapter 15: More Than Just Mechanics: Aesthetics and Longevity

Routine Maintenance for Longevity

Cars, much like us, age with time. Yet, with the right care, they can mature gracefully, continuing to offer reliability and performance long past their expected life spans. Maintaining a vehicle isn't merely a matter of mechanics; it's an ongoing relationship. By committing to routine maintenance, you not only ensure the vehicle's health but also forge a bond that goes beyond metal and oil.

Decoding the Myth of 'Routine'

For many, the term 'routine maintenance' might conjure images of monotonous checklists and frequent trips to the auto shop. But let's demystify this. It's less about sticking to a rigid schedule and more about understanding your car's unique needs.

Listening to Your Car's Whispers

Every car has a language, a series of signs that indicate its current state. It might be the slightly altered hum of the engine or a subtle vibration on the steering wheel. Tuning into these cues can help you address potential issues before they escalate.

For instance, Samantha, a long-time car enthusiast, shared a heartwarming story of her '89 convertible. She'd often drive down to the beach, feeling the wind ruffle through her hair. Over time, she began noticing a soft whirring sound each time she accelerated. Instead of dismissing it, she decided to consult her mechanic. The problem? A minor belt issue. Addressing it promptly not only saved her a potential breakdown in the future but also ensured many more serene drives by the beach.

Fluid Checks: The Lifeblood of Your Car

Much like how our bodies rely on blood, cars lean on various fluids for smooth operation. Regularly checking and replacing these fluids can drastically increase the longevity of your vehicle.

1. **Oil:** Often dubbed the 'blood of the car', motor oil is fundamental. An oil change at regular intervals, depending on the manufacturer's recommendations and driving conditions, can keep your engine running smoothly.

2. **Transmission Fluid:** This ensures that the gear shifts are smooth. Over time, this fluid can degrade, leading to potential transmission issues.

3. **Brake Fluid:** It plays a pivotal role in ensuring that your brakes function correctly. Over time, moisture can infiltrate the brake fluid, reducing its efficacy.

The Subtle Art of Cleaning

Maintaining a car's longevity isn't just about its internal components. Keeping it clean can extend the life of the paint, reduce the risk of rust, and maintain the integrity of the seals.

Imagine the joy of driving a car that not only runs smoothly but also gleams under the sunlight. Nicole, a retired teacher, attributes her car's impeccable condition, even after 15 years, to her bi-weekly cleaning ritual. She believes that this not only keeps the vehicle looking new but also allows her to inspect the car's exterior for any signs of wear and tear.

Bringing in the Experts

While understanding your car and performing minor checks is invaluable, there's no substitute for professional expertise. Scheduling regular service appointments allows experts to inspect your vehicle thoroughly, addressing any underlying issues.

Consider it akin to our routine health check-ups. While daily exercise and a balanced diet keep us in shape, periodic visits to the doctor ensure our well-being. Similarly, while daily care can keep your car in top shape, a mechanic's expert eye can spot and rectify issues we might overlook.

The Bigger Picture: Resale Value and Beyond

Routine maintenance not only ensures a longer life for your vehicle but also affects its resale value. A well-maintained car can command a higher price, making it an investment that bears fruit down the line.

Moreover, the pride of owning a car that stands the test of time, functioning seamlessly year after year, is unparalleled. There's a certain joy in hearing surprised exclamations like, "Wait, your car is *how* old?"

SIX ESSENTIAL FLUIDS TO CHECK IN YOUR CAR

ENGINE OIL

POWER STEERING FLUID

TRANSMISSION FLUID

BRAKE FLUID

COOLANT

WINDSHIELD WIPER FLUID

Protecting and Beautifying Your Vehicle's Exterior

What's the first thing you notice when you see a car? Its color? Its shine? Maybe that little scratch on the door or the tiny rust spot near the wheel? The exterior of a car isn't just about aesthetics. It speaks volumes about the vehicle's history, the adventures it's been on, and, to an extent, the personality of its owner.

The Symphony of Paint and Shine

Cars come with a radiant sheen when they roll off the dealership lot. This is more than just for show. The paint and clear coat serve as the car's armor against external elements. Here's how to ensure it stays vibrant and serves its protective role effectively:

Washing: More than Skin Deep

It's a sunny Sunday afternoon, and you've decided it's time to give your car a good wash. There's more to this ritual than making your vehicle shine.

- **Choosing the Right Soap:** Regular dish soap or detergent can strip the car's paint of its natural oils, leading to dullness over time. Opt for a high-quality car wash soap that's specifically designed to be gentle on your car's paint while effectively removing dirt.

- **The Two-Bucket Method:** Using two buckets, one with soapy water and the other with clean water, ensures that you're not just moving dirt around. After each pass, rinse the cloth in the clean water before dipping it back into the soapy solution.

Waxing: The Shield of Brilliance

Wax isn't just about achieving that magazine-cover shine; it's about protection. Wax provides a barrier against contaminants, UV rays, and light scratches.

- **Frequency Matters:** While there's a satisfying allure to a freshly waxed car, over-waxing isn't beneficial. Depending on the environment and your car's exposure to elements, waxing 2-4 times a year is generally adequate.

- **Choose Your Wax Wisely:** Carnauba-based waxes offer a deep, rich shine and decent protection. Synthetic waxes, on the other hand, may last longer and offer better protection against elements.

Taking Care of Scratches and Dings

Even with the utmost care, life happens. A stray shopping cart or an unfortunately placed bicycle can result in minor scratches and dings.

- **DIY or Professional Help?** For superficial scratches that don't penetrate the paint layer, a DIY approach using scratch remover compounds can be effective. Deeper scratches, however, might require professional touch-ups.

Fighting the Invisible Enemies: Corrosion and Rust

Rust is the silent enemy, gradually eroding the car's bodywork. It's essential to address it at its nascent stage.

- **Regular Inspections:** Make it a habit to inspect areas prone to rust, like the car's underside, wheel wells, and door edges.

- **Immediate Action:** If you spot rust or signs of corrosion, address it immediately. Depending on the severity, you might be able to treat it with anti-rust compounds. In more severe cases, consider seeking professional help.

Accessorizing Thoughtfully

Accessories, like mud flaps, window visors, or even car covers, can offer added protection to your vehicle's exterior. They not only enhance the look but also provide functional benefits. For instance, a car cover is invaluable if you need to park your vehicle outdoors for extended periods.

Beyond Functionality: Infusing Soul into Your Car's Interior

Every time you slide into the driver's seat, grip the steering wheel, or adjust the rear-view mirror, you're stepping into a sanctuary. It's where you belt out your favorite songs, have heart-to-hearts with loved ones, or simply find solace in the hum of the engine and the open road. The car's interior is not just about seats and dashboards; it's about memories and moments.

The Harmony of Comfort and Cleanliness

While the exterior of your car may be its face to the world, the interior is where you spend most of your time. Here's how you can keep it not only clean but inviting and personalized.

Seat Care: Cradles of Comfort

Your seats, whether they're plush fabric or sleek leather, deserve tender loving care. They bear the brunt of daily usage: from the occasional coffee spill to the wear and tear of constant movement.

- **For Fabric Seats:** Vacuuming regularly prevents dirt from embedding into the fibers. Spot-clean spills immediately with a gentle cleaner to prevent stains from setting.

- **For Leather Seats:** Leather needs to breathe. Use dedicated leather cleaners and conditioners to ensure the material remains supple and doesn't crack. Remember, too much direct sunlight can fade and damage leather, so consider using sunshades if you park in exposed areas.

Dashboard and Console: The Heart of Your Car's Interior

Your dashboard isn't just functional; it's the backdrop to many memories.

Keeping it clean and dust-free not only enhances visibility but also adds to the overall driving experience.

- **Regular Dusting:** Using a microfiber cloth, gently wipe the dashboard and console area. These cloths are designed to pick up dust effectively without scratching sensitive surfaces.

- **Protection Against the Sun:** UV rays can cause the dashboard to fade and even crack over time. A dedicated UV protectant spray for car interiors or a simple sunshade can work wonders.

Personal Touches: Making It Uniquely Yours

It's the little things that transform a space from ordinary to personal. Think of the fuzzy dice hanging from the rear-view mirror or the bobblehead on the dashboard.

- **Accessorize with Purpose:** Whether it's seat covers that resonate with your style or a steering wheel cover that feels just right under your palms, choose accessories that enhance comfort and reflect your personality.

- **Scent-sational Vibes:** Scents can powerfully evoke memories. Consider car fresheners or essential oil diffusers to infuse your car's interior with a fragrance that calms, invigorates, or simply makes you smile.

Flooring: The Unsung Hero

Floors might be underfoot, but they're essential. They face muddy shoes, dropped snacks, and the occasional spill.

- **Mats Matter:** Invest in good-quality floor mats. Rubber mats are excellent for rainy or snowy seasons, while carpeted mats can add a touch of luxury.

- **Regular Cleaning:** Every so often, take out the mats, give them a good shake, or even a wash. Vacuum the car's floor to pick up any dirt or debris that's made its way underneath.

Tending to Windows and Mirrors

Streaked windows or foggy mirrors aren't just unsightly; they can be safety hazards.

- **Clean Regularly:** Use an automotive glass cleaner and a microfiber cloth for best results. Remember to clean both the inside and outside of the windows.

- **Fog Management:** If your car windows tend to fog up, consider using anti-fog treatments. Keeping a small squeegee or a defogging pad in the glove compartment can also come in handy.

Your car's interior is an extension of your personal space. It's where countless memories are crafted, from infectious laughter to silent reflections. By maintaining, personalizing, and cherishing this space, you aren't just taking care of a vehicle; you're honoring a repository of stories, journeys, and experiences. Treat it with the love and attention it richly deserve

Conclusion

The Empowered Car Owner: What Lies Ahead

There's an old saying that the journey of a thousand miles begins with a single step. Throughout the course of this book, you've taken not just one step but many strides towards mastering the world of automobiles. With every page turned and every chapter absorbed, you've cultivated a deeper bond with your vehicle, learning to speak its language, understand its needs, and anticipate its wants. Yet, like all profound journeys, this isn't a destination but the beginning of a more significant expedition.

Embracing Mechanical Independence

Mechanical independence isn't about handling every nut and bolt by yourself; it's about understanding. It's about the confidence that emanates from knowing you're in control. The road can be unpredictable. Sometimes, it offers smooth rides under cotton candy skies, and at other times, it challenges with unexpected twists and turns. Being mechanically independent means you're prepared for both.

Redefining the Relationship with Your Vehicle

Cars, for many, are not mere tools for transportation. They are companions on numerous adventures, silent witnesses to our daily lives, and sometimes even the backdrop to life's significant events. By understanding your vehicle's anatomy and nuances, you've transformed the way you perceive it. It's no longer just an assemblage of metal, rubber, and fluids; it's a part of your life's narrative.

The Horizon of Technological Advancements

The auto industry, with its boundless innovations, doesn't stand still. Electric cars, autonomous driving technologies, and vehicles that can communicate with each other are not just the stuff of sci-fi anymore; they are the imminent future. As an empowered car owner, your newfound knowledge sets the stage for you to adapt and evolve with these changes. While technology will continue to redefine mobility, the foundational understanding you've gleaned about vehicles ensures you remain ever relevant and informed.

Beyond the Practical: The Ethos of Care

Cars have stories. The little dent from when you tried to parallel park for the first time, the coffee stain from a memorable road trip, or the scent that instantly transports you to a particular time and place. Your vehicle is an evolving tapestry of memories. The more you care for it, the more stories it gathers, and the longer it stays by your side, making new ones.

Safety, Environment, and the Bigger Picture

With empowerment comes responsibility. An informed car owner isn't just better for their vehicle but for the community and the environment. By ensuring your vehicle is in peak condition, you reduce the risk of accidents, lessen environmental impact, and contribute to a safer road ecosystem for everyone.

Continual Learning: The Road Doesn't End Here

While this guide has equipped you with comprehensive knowledge, remember that learning is a continuous journey. New models, technologies, and techniques emerge regularly. Stay curious, stay engaged, and keep that thirst for knowledge alive. Whether it's subscribing to an automotive magazine, joining a local car enthusiast club, or simply chatting with your mechanic, always be on the lookout for opportunities to learn more.

The Legacy of an Empowered Car Owner

Perhaps years down the line, you'll pass on your car to someone else - maybe a child heading to college, a friend in need, or even trade it in for a newer model. But the stories, memories, and the knowledge stay with you. And these are not just yours to keep but to share. Be the mentor to someone else that this book was to you. Pass on the wisdom, share the anecdotes, and inspire a new generation of empowered car owners.

BONUS Chapter: 15 specific Maintenance Tips

15 Essential Bits Every Car Owner Must Know

The Intimacy of Ownership

Ah, the open road! The thrill of the drive, the hum of the engine, the wind tousling your hair — there's a romance to driving that's hard to put into words. But like any enduring relationship, the bond between a car and its owner isn't just about the grand moments. It's the tiny details, the small learnings, and the day-to-day nuances that truly matter.

The Smell Test: A Whiff of the Unusual

Have you ever paused, sensing an unfamiliar aroma wafting from your vehicle? While it might seem inconsequential, the way your car smells can say a lot. A sweet syrupy scent could mean a coolant leak. The poignant smell of rotten eggs might hint at a problem with your catalytic converter. Being attuned to these olfactory cues can offer timely alerts, potentially saving hefty repair bills.

The Power of Observation: Stains and Spots

Your car might be trying to communicate with you through the stains it leaves behind in your garage. Oil, for instance, will leave a slick brownish stain. A bright green fluid hints at a coolant leak. Paying heed to the colors and consistencies of these telltale droplets can provide insights into the well-being of your car.

A Sound Investment: Tuning in to Noises

While a purring engine is music to the ears, any screeches, whines, or knocks should grab your attention. Whether it's a simple need for lubrication or a deeper mechanical issue, noises often herald the onset of problems. By addressing them early, you can often circumvent more significant challenges down the road.

Your Car's Pulse: Understanding Vibrations

Ever felt an uncanny shake or vibration while cruising? It could be as mundane as needing a wheel balance, or it might be hinting at more pressing issues like brake problems or drivetrain issues. Recognizing these vibrations early can be key to diagnosing and addressing problems before they escalate.

The Virtue of Patience: Warming Up Your Engine
In an age of instant gratification, it's tempting to roar away as soon as you start the engine. However, giving your vehicle a minute to warm up, especially during colder months, can go a long way in ensuring its longevity.

A Matter of Balance: Tire Pressures and Perils
It's not just about avoiding flats. Maintaining optimal tire pressure impacts fuel efficiency, handling, and overall safety. A simple pressure gauge and regular checks can make a world of difference in your driving experience.

Reading the Signs: The Tale of the Tachometer
While speedometers get all the attention, the tachometer (measuring engine RPMs) is an unsung hero. By ensuring your engine isn't overworked, especially during highway driving, you not only boost performance but also avoid undue wear and tear.

Peek Under the Hood: Regular Under-the-Hood Checks
Beyond the regular maintenance, a sporadic glance under the hood can be enlightening. Check for frayed belts, any signs of leaks, or damaged pipes. This isn't about playing mechanic but about being an observant owner.

Fluid Dynamics: The Lifeblood of Your Car
Oil isn't the only fluid your car thrives on. Brake fluid, transmission fluid, power steering fluid - all play pivotal roles. Ensuring they're at the right levels and get changed at the right intervals is essential.

Shady Business: Using Your Vehicle's Shade
Parking in the shade isn't just about keeping the car cool. Constant exposure to direct sunlight can take a toll on the car's paint job and interiors. Whenever possible, opt for a shady spot or use sun shades to protect your vehicle.

Being Grounded: The Importance of a Clean Ground Connection
Electrical issues can be a driver's nightmare. One often overlooked aspect is ensuring a clean and robust ground connection for your vehicle's electrical system. Periodic checks can stave off a host of electrical problems.

All About Timing: Synchronizing Your Engine's Ballet
The timing belt is like the conductor of an orchestra, ensuring every component works in harmony. Knowing when it's due for a replacement can prevent sudden breakdowns and expensive engine repairs.

Venturing Out: The Value of Occasional Long Drives
While short commutes are the norm, an occasional long drive can do wonders for your car. It can help clear out carbon build-ups, recharge the battery, and ensure various parts get a thorough workout.

A Clean Slate: Regular Car Washes and Their Impact
Beyond aesthetics, regular car washes remove grit, bird droppings, and other contaminants that can wear down paint and lead to rust. A clean car isn't just about pride but about preservation.

Made in the USA
Coppell, TX
23 November 2024